Protecting Children

a guide for sportspeople

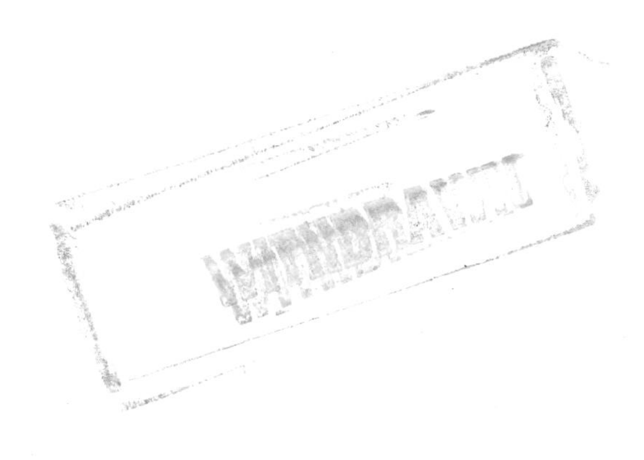

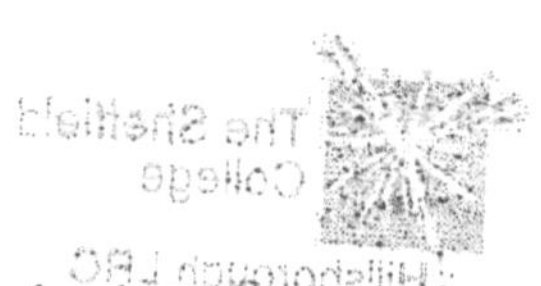

ISBN 0 947850 50 3

sports coach UK
114 Cardigan Road
Headingley
Leeds LS6 3BJ
Tel: 0113-274 4802 Fax: 0113-275 5019
E-mail: coaching@sportscoachuk.org Website: www.sportscoachuk.org

Patron: HRH The Princess Royal

First and second editions

Developed from an original text by Maureen Crouch (NSPCC) in conjunction with the Royal Yachting Association (RYA) and edited by Penny Crisfield (NCF)

Third edition

Author
Gil Lester

Editors
Nicola Cooke, Lucy Williams

Sub-editor
Ian Smyth

Typesetter
Sandra Flintham

The publishers would like to thank the following for their valuable input to this handbook:
Steve Boocock, Tim Gardner, Andy Rangecroft, Biddy Rowe, Hamish Telfer

Cover photo
sports coach UK

Published on behalf of **sports coach UK** by
Coachwise Solutions
Chelsea Close
Off Amberley Road
Armley
Leeds LS12 4HP
Tel: 0113-231 1310 Fax: 0113-231 9606
E-mail: enquiries@coachwise.ltd.uk Website: www.coachwisesolutions.co.uk

Preface

In 2001, Government figures indicated that over 34,000[1] children were officially registered as being in need of protection from abuse. The unofficial estimate of children in need of protection is many thousands more. Children may be abused regardless of their age, race, gender, culture, religious belief, disability or sexual identity. They are usually abused by people they know and trust – these could be people from inside or outside the family. As yet, no figures relating specifically to sport are available. However, the fact that there are known cases of abuse in sport is evidence enough. Every possible measure should therefore be taken to ensure that sport is a safe experience for children[2].

People who work with children in sport on a regular basis may be able to provide an important link in identifying a child who has been, or is, at risk of being harmed. Therefore, all those directly or indirectly involved with children's sport have a responsibility to:

- review their own practice in sport situations to ensure that it complies with advocated and recognised codes of conduct
- explore their own values and attitudes in relation to child abuse
- be informed and able to recognise signs and symptoms of child abuse
- respond in an appropriate way to children who disclose they are being abused
- take appropriate action if concerns are raised which suggest a child is being abused.

---

1 NSPCC figures, based on statistics for England, Northern Ireland and Wales.

2 In the context of this pack, the term *children* is used to refer to children and young people up to the age of 18, and vulnerable adults who may have specific needs.

sports coach UK is committed to raising awareness of, and implementing action plans, for child protection in sport. Although the emphasis of *Protecting Children: A Guide for Sportspeople* is on coaching, the pack is aimed at all those with responsibility for the organisation of children's sport (eg national governing bodies[1], local authorities, centre managers, sports clubs) and those who lead or deliver children's sport programmes (eg coaches, leaders, teachers, instructors, development officers, officials, administrators, volunteers, parents).[2]

This pack is **not** intended as an expert's comprehensive manual. Instead it offers a practical guide for all those involved in sport for children. It aims to increase awareness about child abuse and help you to recognise the signs of abuse and deal sensitively and effectively with the issue should it arise. It also prompts you to review your own practice to ensure that sport provides a positive and enriching experience for children and that your behaviour is always above reproach.

By the end of this pack, you should be able to:

- identify the foundations of good practice and child protection
- describe the different categories of child abuse
- recognise the signs and symptoms of each category
- identify appropriate action to take if abuse is suspected
- recognise the roles and responsibilities of other agencies/organisations.

In the context of coaching, *Protecting Children: A Guide for Sportspeople* will encourage you to consider the issues you may encounter when coaching children and, most importantly, to explore what good coaching practice involves. It provides the essential information required to enable you to meet the minimum standards of the *Active Sports Programme*[3]. The pack also supports a three-hour **sports coach UK** workshop[4], which you are strongly recommended to attend. This will help you put the theory behind child protection into practice and apply it to your own coaching.

You may have had some training and/or experience in child protection already. In this case, this pack will help you to think more about your responsibilities in sport settings and how you may share your knowledge and experience with others. However, you may have had no previous experience in this area and may want to spend more time on some sections than others, or discuss issues with your colleagues.

---

1 In the context of this pack, the term *national governing body* is used to refer to all organisations with responsibility for overseeing the policies and affairs of sport.

2 In the context of this pack, the term *coach* is used to refer to any of the groups of people listed in this paragraph.

3 The Active Programme is one of Sport England's major programmes focusing on getting more people involved in sport. It consists of three main elements – Active Sports, Active Schools and Active Communities.

4 For further details, contact the Workshop Booking Centre on 0845-601 3054.

Although this pack is designed for you to work through on your own or as a follow-up to the accompanying workshop, some of the issues covered may raise strong feelings for you. It might be helpful to identify someone who is also working through the pack with whom you can meet regularly to share your thoughts. Make sure you have a clear agreement about how you will work together. Additionally, if you are unsure about the issues raised, you should make a note and discuss these with relevant staff in your club/organisation (eg line manager, director of coaching, centre manager) or seek further support from the agencies listed on pages 120 to 122.

Key to symbols used in the text	
	Activity
	Stop and consider
	Important information
	Points of interest
	Remember

Throughout this pack, the pronouns he, she, him, her and so on are interchangeable and intended to be inclusive of both males and females. It is important in sport, as elsewhere, that both genders have equal status and opportunities.

Contents

Section One – The Foundations of Good Practice and Child Protection

Section Two – Understanding and Identifying Signs of Child Abuse

Section Three – Taking Appropriate Action

Section Four – Where Next?

Section Five – Appendices

Section One

The Foundations of Good Practice and Child Protection

1.0 Introduction

Sport can have a very powerful and positive influence on people – especially children – and should provide opportunities for both enjoyment and achievement. Through sport, children can develop valuable qualities such as leadership, confidence and self-esteem.

However, these positive outcomes can only be achieved if the coaching you provide is of the highest possible standard. It is essential that you understand and act on your responsibilities, so that children can enjoy sport within a safe and secure environment where they feel protected and empowered to make the most suitable choices. Providing children with positive sporting experiences means that they will be more likely to achieve their true potential.

This first section will introduce you to the key principles of good coaching practice and relate these specifically to the context of coaching children. As you work through the section, you may well identify aspects of good practice that you already adopt in your work; you may also encounter other issues that have not occurred to you before, but which you may need to address when coaching children in the future.

By the end of this section you should be able to explain the:

- key principles of **sports coach** UK's (scUK's) *Code of Conduct for Sports Coaches*
- implications of these principles for:
  - coaching in general
  - your club/organisation
  - coaching children.

1.1 Code of Conduct for Sports Coaches

In any profession, whether paid or voluntary, there are accepted and established codes of behaviour. For example, doctors and solicitors are required to conform to a professional code of practice. Many companies and organisations now adopt customer charters (eg The Patient's Charter) to ensure the needs of the customer are kept paramount at all times. Such codes exist to safeguard the welfare of the customer and to protect the service provider from false allegations.

A code of conduct is just as necessary in coaching as in any other profession. This was first recognised by the National Coaching Foundation[1] in 1995 with the publication of its *Code of Ethics and Conduct for Sports Coaches*, which was based on an original code drawn up by the British Institute of Sports Coaches. Revised in 2001, this subsequently became **scUK**'s *Code of Conduct for Sports Coaches*. The following extract from the revised code emphasises the need for a code of conduct in coaching:

Coaching, as an emerging profession, must demonstrate at all levels a high degree of honesty, integrity and competence. The need for coaches to understand and act on their responsibilities is of critical importance to sport, as is the need to protect the key concept of participation for fun and enjoyment as well as achievement. This is implicit within good coaching practice and promotes a professional image of the good practitioner. This code of conduct defines all that is best in good coaching practice.

Code of Conduct for Sports Coaches (2001)[2]

1 **sports coach UK** (**scUK**) since April 2001.

2 Available from Coachwise Ltd (Tel 0113-231 1310 or visit www.1st4sport.com).

The *Code of Conduct for Sports Coaches* has been adopted by a number of national governing bodies and educational providers providing both academic and vocational sports courses. All **scUK** members[1] must agree to abide by the Code themselves as well as to promote it to all others involved in coaching.

The Code is based around the four key principles described in the panel below:

Code of Conduct for Sports Coaches – Key Principles

Rights – coaches must respect and champion the rights of every individual to participate in sport.

Relationships – coaches must develop a relationship with athletes (and others) based on openness, honesty, mutual trust and respect.

Responsibilities: personal standards – coaches must demonstrate proper personal behaviour and conduct at all times.

Responsibilities: professional standards – to maximise benefits and minimise the risks to athletes, coaches must attain a high level of competence through qualifications and a commitment to ongoing training that ensures safe and correct practice.

Code of Conduct for Sports Coaches (2001)

These key principles relate to the relationship between coaches and performers. They may also apply to relationships with other people, including parents, guardians, friends, peers, teachers, medics and the press. This list should be an active one, changing as the coaching process develops and as coaches view each performer within their individual sporting environment.

The key principles apply in any coaching situation, whatever the specific role of coaches within their club/organisation, but are particularly important when coaching children. However, they do not apply exclusively to coaches, but to all those working with children in a sporting environment.

1 **scUK** membership services provide access to benefits and information for anyone with an interest in sport and coaching, and additional specific benefits for qualified sports coaches. For further details, telephone 0113-278 4802 or visit www.sportscoachuk.org

1.2 Implications for Coaching

Section 1.1 introduced you to the four key principles of **scUK**'s *Code of Conduct for Sports Coaches*. This section will explore the implications of these principles for coaching.

While the principles affect coaching in general, they are particularly important when coaching children. Children therefore feature in some of the scenarios in the activities so that you can start to focus on this area of coaching. In the activities, you will be asked to evaluate the actions of coaches in specific scenarios as well as consider what you would do in certain situations. As a result, you should begin to think about how to integrate the four key principles into your own coaching practice.

Rights

In order to respect and champion the rights of every individual to participate in sport, you should:

- provide choices for individual performers in your sport or activity
- provide an environment in which children are free from fear or harassment
- recognise the rights of performers to be treated as individuals
- encourage performers to confer with other coaches or experts if the need arises
- promote the concept of a well-balanced lifestyle for performers both within and outside of sport.

ACTIVITY 1

The aim of this activity is to focus your thoughts on player rights. In each of the scenarios in the table opposite, the coach seems to have forgotten how to be a professional. Consider how he or she could have handled the situation better and note your ideas in the right-hand column.

	Scenario	More Acceptable Solution
1	Ali books a place on a tennis course. On arriving at the first session, it's obvious the course is very popular and that all the courts are already full. The coach looks a bit flustered and sends Ali away to play rounders until a court becomes available. He doesn't appear to have a register – in fact, he doesn't really seem familiar with the tennis course programme at all.	
2	Satu's mother signs her up for a girls-only swimming class, as Satu doesn't want to take part in a mixed class. However, due to a lack of pool availability, the coach combines the girls-only class with a mixed club training session. She thinks it will be possible to run both sessions at the same time, without the groups getting in each other's way.	
3	Moya needs to take time out from a busy training schedule to observe a religious festival. His coach is not pleased and says that Moya will lose his place in the team as a result. Several other team members also have religious festivals to observe, but feel unable to say so. The coach doesn't provide an alternative for the children concerned and says that she is not prepared to tolerate those who do not put their training first.	
4	After a close match, Jimmy is blamed for the team losing. His coach later tells other team members that Jimmy is overweight and should go on a diet.	
5	After a tournament, a coach provides feedback that reduces many of her team members to tears. They were up against some stiff competition and played as well as possible. The other teams all hear what is said and feel embarrassed for them.	

Now turn over.

Feedback

Scenario 1

Ali may have been upset by the fact that the coach didn't seem to be expecting him and failed to welcome him to the course. Playing a game of rounders is not a suitable alternative. Ali has booked his place on the tennis course – the coach's solution in this case means that the agreed service has not been provided. As a coach, it is important to consider issues such as resources, facilities and special needs before a session begins.

Scenario 2

In this case, Satu's mother's personal beliefs will not allow her daughter to take part in a mixed class. Deciding that an excellent alternative would be to allow Satu to swim with a girls-only class, she has booked this class in advance. It is not until she arrives at the swimming pool that Satu discovers she cannot attend the class on offer. The coach should have advised Satu's mother of any changes prior to the class being held.

Scenario 3

This is a difficult situation, but no child should be penalised as a result of his/her religious beliefs. If the coach maintains this attitude, the children concerned may decide to drop out of the team and the coach may be considered a bully. Under the terms of the Children Act 1989, all children have the right to be consulted about what they want to do.

Scenario 4

If a coach attempts to lay blame in this way, he is acting in an unprofessional manner. If Jimmy is overweight, the coach should direct him to expert help rather than to make him feel like a victim in front of his fellow team members. This may result in Jimmy giving up the sport with memories of a negative experience.

Scenario 5

Although it is natural for children to get upset if they are given negative feedback, you should never give feedback that is intended to cause upset or humiliation in front of others. Instead, it is important to learn how to provide constructive criticism. This approach will allow children to both acknowledge their strengths and consider how they could improve their performance in future matches.

Remember!

Sport should always be a positive experience for all children. You should:

- *treat all individuals in sport with respect at all times*
- *not discriminate on the grounds of gender, marital status, race, colour, disability, sexuality, age, occupation, religion or political opinion*
- *not condone, or allow to go unchallenged, any form of discrimination*
- *not publicly criticise or engage in demeaning descriptions of others*
- *be discreet in any conversations about performers, coaches or other individuals*
- *communicate with, and provide feedback to, performers in a manner which reflects respect and care.*

You may feel that there are further issues to consider in relation to player rights – include these in your club's/organisation's own code of conduct[1].

sports coach UK

1 See page 14 for further details.

Relationships

As a coach, you must develop relationships with children and others that are based on openness, honesty, mutual trust and respect.

You should always:

- consider your behaviour – do not engage in behaviour that constitutes any form of abuse
- promote the welfare and best interests of your performers, even if this means letting another professional *take over*
- avoid sexual intimacy with performers at all times and under any conditions, including immediately after the coaching relationship has ended
- empower performers to be responsible for their own decisions
- clarify the nature of the coaching services being offered to performers
- communicate and cooperate with other organisations and individuals in the best interests of your performers.

ACTIVITY 2

The aim of this activity is to apply the relationship principles described above to your own coaching environment. Consider how you would approach each of the aspects of coaching listed in the left-hand column of the table on page 9 in your sport and note your ideas in the right-hand column. An example of each aspect is provided in the middle column to help you put it into the context of coaching children.

Note: Remember that what constitutes good practice in one sport may be deemed inappropriate in another. You may need to consult with national governing bodies or seek further clarification from a sport-specific development officer. If necessary, explain how the code of practice or guidelines would vary for different performance levels and in different sports.

Aspect of Coaching	Example	Your Specific Code of Practice or Guidelines
Physical Contact	For safety reasons, you may need to lift or support a child as he performs a particular technique – your national governing body should be able to provide specific guidelines.	
Training Practices	Your sport may require children to participate in weight-bearing activities – your national governing body should be able to provide specific guidelines.	
Language	You may need to use technical language that is difficult for children to either understand or use – it's a good idea to provide a glossary of terms that they can refer to.	
Player Welfare	You may need to consider issues such as player diet or consumption of alcohol – it's a good idea to discuss this with children's parents or carers.	
Coaching Services	You could find that a child needs medical treatment after taking part in your training session – it's a good idea to meet their parents or carers to discuss issues such as recommended sports therapists or training implications.	

Now turn over.

Feedback

- **Physical contact**
  It is good practice for coaches to inform children, parents and carers that, in some sports, it will be essential for the coach to manually support the child in order for them to perform a technique safely. If this applies to you, you should outline the nature of the support and any further actions that may be necessary if the child needs additional help to perform the technique safely.

- **Training practices**
  In some sports, you may need to explain training practices in detail so that everyone involved in the coaching process understands exactly why and when factors relating to intensity, duration, nutrition or treatment are important.

- **Language**
  Always consider the age and experience of the children you are working with. In some cases, it may be appropriate to use technical terminology (when children need to learn the specifics of movements, tactics and rules); in other cases, you may need to simplify the terminology used. Remember that the meaning attached to certain words may vary from region to region. You should try to ensure that the language you use does not confuse children; it should not be a barrier to their understanding and enjoyment of sport.

- **Player welfare**
  The relationship between the child as a young performer and the child as someone who is able to make decisions relating to their own training, is straightforward in some cases and more delicate in others. You should encourage children to take responsibility for their own development and actions.

- **Coaching services**
  You should discuss and agree on experts or organisations that can offer appropriate further services, with the child and/or parents or carers. Always inform the child and/or parent or carer of any potential costs involved.

Responsibilities

You will often find yourself in positions of considerable influence – particularly when coaching children. You therefore have a profound responsibility to demonstrate and set high moral and ethical standards throughout your coaching practice. Your primary role is to improve performance and to demonstrate proper personal behaviour and conduct at all times.

Remember!

You should always:

- be fair, honest and considerate to performers and others in your sport
- project an image of health, cleanliness and functional efficiency
- be a positive role model for performers at all times.

ACTIVITY 3

As a coach, you have a responsibility to review and examine your behaviour constantly to ensure that it conforms to good practice and cannot be misconstrued.

1. With reference to responsibility and professional standards, jot down the issues you would expect to consider both before and during a coaching session in the left-hand column of the table below.
2. In the right-hand column, note the action you would take (ie what you would do and/or think about) to ensure good practice.

Issues to Consider	Action Required

Now turn over.

Feedback

You may have listed some or all of the following issues:

- *Health*
- *Safety*
- *Insurance*
- *Risk assessment*
- *Paperwork*
- *Incident forms*
- *Consent checks*
- *Phone numbers*
- *Professional qualifications*
- *Being a role model*
- *Standards of dress and behaviour*
- *Coach burnout*
- *Data Protection Act*
- *Photography*
- *References*
- *Links with others*
- *Driving insurance*
- *First aid.*

Summary

Good coaching practice involves:

- promoting safe and correct practice in relation to:
  - physical environment
  - other performers
  - significant others (eg umpires, drivers, ground staff)
- accepting professional responsibility for your actions
- making a commitment to provide a high quality of service
- providing a positive benefit to society through sport
- acknowledging that sport is a developing profession and that it is important to exchange knowledge and best practice tips
- working towards coaching qualifications at different levels.

The table below lists four key actions that will help to ensure good practice in your coaching, together with examples.

Action	Examples
Follow national governing body/employer guidelines	• Attend courses • Gather essential information • Keep abreast of new developments • Maintain professional level of coaching • Make use of educational opportunities
Locate support services in your area	• Other clubs/coaches • Sports development officers • Injury/treatment referral • Specific expertise (eg elite level or disability sport) • Local/national squads • Trials • Schools
Check your own coaching practice	• Appraisal/analysis • Mentor system • Session planning • Workload • Home demands • Own health/lifestyle
Review the social issues surrounding your sport	• Local, regional or national initiatives • Methods of fund-raising/grants/lottery funding • Rewarding teams, individuals • Training weekends, camps, tours

You may like to share your thoughts and ideas with other professionals, colleagues and friends. The process of providing good practice in coaching is a continually developing one and depends on the cooperation and dedication of others.

1.3 Implications for Your Club/Organisation

This section outlines measures your club/organisation can take to promote the key principles outlined in Sections 1.1 and 1.2, and thus provide a safe sporting environment for children.

Developing a Code of Conduct

In the UK, steps are being taken to ensure that codes of conduct are incorporated into national governing body and employer constitutions. Opportunities are now available for an individual, club/organisation or local authority to fully implement good practice within their coaching programmes. This may involve:

- an accreditation process
- a coach education programme
- a commitment to implement policies and procedures
- accessing central information systems (eg local authorities, national governing bodies, Criminal Records Bureau).

Use the key principles of **scUK**'s *Code of Conduct for Sports Coaches* as the basis for a code of conduct for your club/organisation:

- Begin with a policy statement that recognises the four key principles introduced on page 3.
- Outline the importance of relationships among all those involved in the coaching process and relate these to your club's/organisation's environment.
- If appropriate, involve others such as parents, volunteers, and teachers or, for elite performers, advanced coaches. You may also wish to consult your performers to decide exactly what is acceptable and what is not.
- Amend and update your code regularly to ensure that sport continues to be a safe and fun experience for all those involved.
- Consider developing separate codes of conduct for different groups of people (eg players, referees, umpires, parents, and supporters).

Inevitably, all codes of conduct have their limitations – to be effective, the key principles must be acknowledged and adopted by all those involved. The aim of the next activity is to illustrate the importance of ensuring that good practice is embedded within the working practices of your entire club/organisation. Taking responsibility for this will not only help your club/organisation to promote a professional image, but is also vital to the future of sport.

ACTIVITY 4

In the space provided below, draw a diagram which identifies all the people within your club/organisation that you would need to consult when relating the key principles outlined on page 3 to the context of coaching children. It may help to place the child at the centre of your diagram and to then consider everyone who will come into direct or indirect contact with her.

Now turn over.

Feedback

Good practice involves seeking support when you need it. *As a coach, you should never feel that you are alone – you should feel able to seek help, advice or support whenever it may help you deal with an issue.*

Your diagram may have included some, or all of, the following groups of people. You may like to use the spaces provided to note the names and telephone numbers of specific people in your club/organisation or local area to whom you may turn for help and support.

People Who May Help	Name(s)	Tel No
Other coaches in your club/organisation		
Other coaches in your local area		
Friends		
Your line manager		
Head coach		
Development officer/sports development officer		
County development officer		
Regional organiser		
National governing body		
Local leisure authority		
Club committee		
Club employees/caretaker/groundsman		
Parents		
Doctor/dentist		
Police		
Emergency services (eg fire, rescue, hospital)		
Insurance company		
Local newspaper		

Recruitment, Employment and Deployment of Staff

Your club's/organisation's policy and/or code of conduct should clearly state that all reasonable steps will be taken to ensure that unsuitable people are prevented from working with children. The checklist below and on page 18 covers the main issues to consider when recruiting staff or volunteers.

Checklist for the Recruitment, Employment and Deployment of Staff and Volunteers

Pre-recruitment

1. Determine the aims of your club/organisation and, if possible, the particular sports programme that you wish to staff.
2. Identify the responsibilities that the member of staff will be expected to have.
3. Determine the level of experience or qualifications required, taking into account any national governing body and/or local authority guidelines.
4. Outline your club's/organisation's open and positive stance on child protection.
5. Formalise your advertising procedure.
6. Prepare a job description – include roles and responsibilities.
7. Write a person specification.
8. Prepare an application form asking applicants to provide the following details:
   - Name, address and National Insurance number
   - Relevant experience, qualifications, training
   - Past career or involvement in sport
   - Any criminal record
   - A self-disclosure section to establish whether any action has been taken against them in relation to child abuse, sexual offences or violence
   - The names of two people (not relatives) willing to provide written references that comment on the applicant's previous experience of, and suitability for, working with children – previous employer is preferable
   - The applicant's consent to criminal record checks being undertaken if necessary
   - The applicant's consent to abide by the club's/organisation's code of conduct appropriate to the position sought.

Forms should also state that failure to disclose information or subsequent failure to conform to the code of conduct will result in disciplinary action and possible exclusion from the club/organisation.

Interview

In certain circumstances, it may be appropriate to conduct a formal interview. Ensure that it is conducted in accordance with appropriate interview protocol.

Checks

- A minimum of two written references should be requested, one of which should be from a previous employer. All references should be followed up and confirmed by telephone.
- If the applicant has qualifications, ask to see appropriate evidence (eg certificates).
- If the applicant has no previous experience of working with children, recommend that they seek appropriate training.
- You may wish to conduct criminal record checks to assess the suitability of the applicant to work with children. This can be done via the:
  - Criminal Records Bureau (England and Wales)[1]
  - Scottish Office, Social Work Services Group (Scotland)
  - DHSSPS Pre-Employment Consultancy Service (PECS) (Northern Ireland).

Training

- Ensure that all new members of staff receive a formal induction to your club/organisation (eg introduction to your facility, basic procedures such as fire drills, safety, and first aid).
- All staff working with children are recommended to receive training in the following areas[2]:
  - Child protection awareness
  - First aid
  - Working effectively with children
  - Child-centred coaching styles.

It is also essential that staff receive regular, follow-up training to ensure that they are kept up to date with current issues.

Monitoring and Appraisal

All staff or volunteers should be given the opportunity to receive formal or informal feedback (eg at the end of a particular sports programme or at regular intervals during an ongoing programme).

Complaints

Check that your organisation or club has a formal complaints procedure.

---

1 See Appendix A for further details.

2 **scUK** offers a wide range of workshops and supporting packs in a variety of coaching-related areas. Telephone 0113-274 4802 or visit www.sportscoachuk.org for further details.

ACTIVITY 5

Comment on the guidelines on pages 17 to 18. Are they realistic? Are they achievable? Could you suggest further areas for development within your organisation?

Communication

Good communication is vital to the effective operation of your club/organisation in general, but is particularly important in the context of coaching children.

Establishing and maintaining effective communication channels in your club/organisation could involve:

- publishing a newsletter
- organising fund-raising activities
- setting up a committee
- establishing a supporters' club
- setting up a lottery panel
- establishing and maintaining a link with the local sports development officer
- providing a coach education programme
- providing in-house training/development opportunities.

Many clubs/organisations have implemented systems through which to share good practice and to provide coach feedback through formal channels. With such a system in place, managers should be able to identify concerns that could be addressed by a coach education programme or a simple change of coaching focus.

Examples of Good Practice

The next activity asks you to identify examples of good practice at a fictional sports club. Some of these may already exist in your club/organisation; others may be things you hadn't necessarily thought of before.

ACTIVITY 6

Read through the following scenario. As you do, jot down any examples of good practice that you come across.

A number of improvements have been made to Parkgate Sports Club over the past few months. These include the installation of a free drinking water fountain, a telephone from which club members can make free local calls, security lighting and the services of a night security agency.

The club committee already runs a number of activity schemes and systematically reviews both the quality and scope of provision. All committee members have attended a range of sports administration courses and support the various activity schemes in their capacity as volunteer coaches. The full-time coaching officer is responsible for planning a programme of activities for the entire summer holiday, ensuring adequate staffing arrangements and for the behaviour and standards of the club's coaches.

The next plan of action is to organise a sports play scheme during a school holiday for local children aged seven to fourteen. At the first committee meeting, roles and responsibilities are allocated to committee members in order to recruit staff to provide a range of indoor and outdoor activities.

An advert is subsequently placed in a local newspaper. All applicants are required to complete an application form, attend an interview and supply two references. All successful applicants are asked to attend formal induction programmes at the club and are employed on short-term contracts.

With all staff members recruited, children are invited to enrol on the play scheme. All of them are asked to complete appropriate registration documents and to attend an orientation session during which club rules and regulations are explained. Parents are invited to attend at least one orientation session per family of children and to meet all club staff. The club operates an inclusion policy and does all it can to cater for members' specific needs as and when required.

Every day, one of the committee members is on duty and responsible, not just for general duties, but also for checking facilities and equipment. During activity sessions the club is closed with entry via a main reception area. Children also use this system to check in and leave. The club encourages parents/carers or a named person to collect their children at the end of their session. Children are invited to provide feedback (either after a specific session or on a weekly basis) and have access to non-coaching volunteers for queries. All courses are reviewed on a regular basis in terms of attendance and quality.

Now turn over.

Feedback

The committee at Parkgate Sports Club has made every effort to provide a high quality programme of activities for children which meets standards of good practice.

The many examples of good practice demonstrated in the scenario should contribute to the provision of a positive sporting environment for children – these include:

- *providing good club facilities (eg drinking water, telephone, security lighting, overnight security guard)*
- *not only having a club committee, but having one that is committed to supporting staff, meeting customer needs and providing a safe, secure environment*
- *reviewing previous activities to identify examples of good practice and areas for improvement*
- *providing training for committee members and staff*
- *having a designated coaching officer responsible for planning the club's programme of activities*
- *providing activities for different age groups*
- *allocating roles and responsibilities to specific staff*
- *having formal recruitment and induction procedures*
- *keeping records of children attending the club*
- *providing orientation sessions for children and their parents/carers*
- *making every effort to be equitable and to cater for all children, even those with specific needs*
- *carrying out risk assessments of activities, resources and equipment*
- *controlling the arrival and departure of people at the club and keeping a register of attendance*
- *obtaining and acting on customer feedback.*

1.4 Implications for Coaching Children

It is essential that a culture of honesty, integrity and competence exists in coaching. This means:

- understanding and acting on your responsibilities as a coach
- recognising the need to protect the key concept of participation for fun and enjoyment as well as achievement.

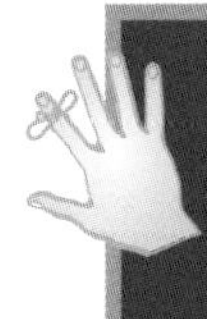

Remember!
All staff, including coaches who work independently, should not only be required to sign up to your club's/organisation's code of conduct, but to also ensure that they demonstrate good practice at all times.

Acting as a Role Model

Not all children may behave as you would like during your coaching sessions. Often, they are influenced by the media's portrayal of their professional sports stars heroes. Unfortunately, the media tend to focus on incidents of poor, rather than good, behaviour and often blow things out of proportion. However, children are unlikely to understand this and may try to emulate undesirable behaviour that they have witnessed in major matches or events. This may result in a conflict between you and the children, and if ignored, could have disastrous consequences.

sports coach UK

As a coach, you should always try to be a positive role model for the children you coach on the basis that, if you act in a responsible manner, they will be encouraged to do so too. Following the tips in the panel below will help you to do this:

- **Appearance** – always project a professional image.
- **Fashion** – you don't have to be a fashion model, but you do need to meet certain standards in terms of appropriate kit and equipment.
- **Tattoos** – very popular but not always desirable.
- **Jewellery** – remove, or at least tape up, any jewellery during sport.
- **Language** – it is often not just what is said that is important, but how it is said. Never use foul language in front of the children you coach.
- **Alcohol** –it is unacceptable to consume, or be under the influence of, alcohol when responsible for children.
- **Drugs** – take a firm stance against drugs and lead by example.

Action Plus

ACTIVITY 7

Read through the following scenario:

Your team has reached the final of a local competition. On the day of the match, several supporters turn up to watch, so the atmosphere is noisy and the team members are very excited. You know the referee and you instruct your team to play fair, but hard. You emphasise that the referee is tough and that they will have to watch their language, tackles and general behaviour. However, you are very pleased that they have reached this far in the competition and find it difficult not to concentrate just on winning.

During the first half, the score is even and the crowd is satisfied with the general play and the referee's decisions. However, due to a poor tackle from a member of the other team late in the first half, your best player has to leave the pitch injured. Soon after this, the other team scores and takes the lead. You see that your players are demoralised, tired and desperate to equalise. It is at this point that you notice the standard of their play deteriorates – you also spot incidents of shirt pulling, late tackles and offensive language.

In the space provided below, explain what you would do during half-time to re-focus your players. What would you say to them?

Now turn over.

Feedback

This is a very common situation. Young or inexperienced players may often feel that the only way to win is to copy poor behaviour that they have seen elsewhere. In this example, the players on the coach's team felt that they were not going to win without resorting to desperate measures – even though they could be considered to be cheating. They feel that if they 'cheat', they will score goals. They do not associate the concept of 'fair play' with their present situation but are only focused on the idea of winning.

Empowering Children

As a coach – particularly of children – you hold a powerful and unique leadership role, often carrying considerable authority and status. This role is frequently accompanied by a closeness and mutual trust usually held only between the parent and the child. You often wittingly or unwittingly assume this level of authority, and occasionally your influence spills over into the child's personal life. One of the challenges you repeatedly face is to manage this potential power and to balance the responsible and safe boundary between coach and performer. The challenge to do this is exacerbated by the need for you to build high levels of trust from children – particularly those involved in elite performance – in order to encourage them to optimise their performance and develop the level of commitment required to achieve their potential.

When coaching children, you may start by using your authoritative role to build a strong relationship or bond. This can, and often does, result in you having a very positive influence over the child – sometimes an influence that grows even more powerful than that of the child's parents or schoolteachers. Over time, the all-important trust needed normally develops.

However, with this trust comes increased vulnerability and the potential for you to misuse or even abuse your power. This might be the result of thoughtlessness, negligence or, occasionally, wickedness. Even a passive type of abuse of power (questioning a child's loyalty or commitment) may enhance the child's need for belonging. Over time, this may result in over-conformity, obsessive behaviours and emotional dependency.

As you become important in the development of a child, you may need to examine your own coaching behaviour. Likewise, the child may develop an attraction for you based on a misunderstanding through such a close relationship. Care should be taken that the relationship is a positive one and not one that could be misinterpreted by others.

There is, of course, a close but potentially dangerous relationship between commitment and conformity. Inadvertently (or intentionally), you may encourage conformity to your values and ideals of commitment to sport. In seeking greater sporting commitment, you may therefore be over-stressing the need to conform and possibly thwarting personal responsibility and self-determination, thus encouraging over-dependence in the child. It is important to recognise and avoid the potential negative consequences of power and trust. Your role as a coach should be to instil confidence in the children you coach, so that they are willing to play an active role in the coaching process.

Figure 1 below illustrates responsible leadership. Try to relate it to your own coaching. How well do you manage your relationships with your own performers?

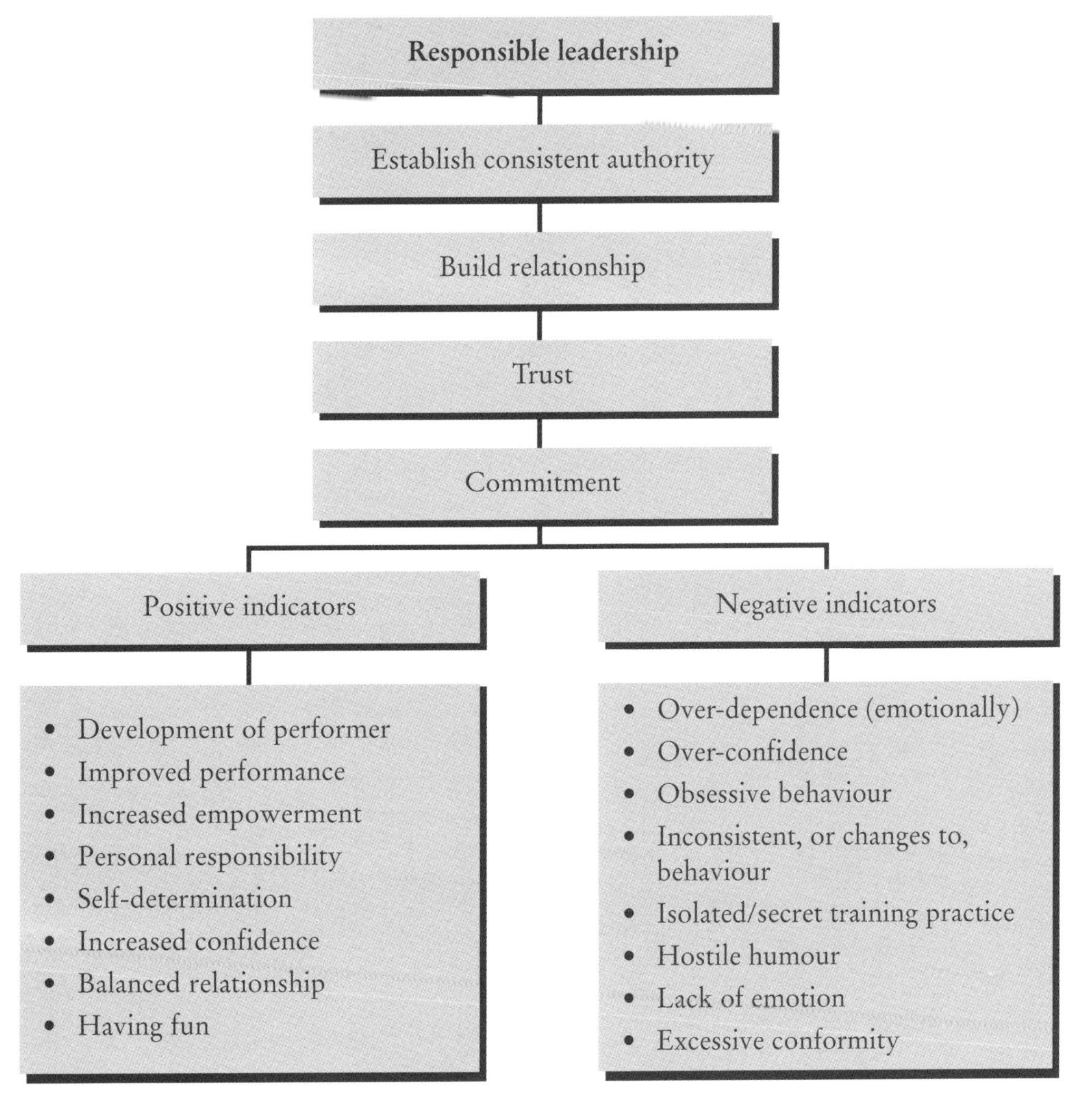

Figure 1: Responsible leadership

Adopting Good Practice

You should try to compile a list of actions that will help you become child-focused and ensure good practice and standards. This should be an active list and should be constantly updated in line with the changing coaching environment, a variety of social needs, your own expectations and the demands of others.

ACTIVITY 8

The *good practice tool box* in the left-hand column of the table below contains examples of good practice that you should try to adopt in your coaching practice. In the right-hand column, jot down ways in which you could do this. If you can, add extra examples of good practice in the spaces provided at the end of the table (on page 30).

Good Practice Tool Box	Action Points
Make sport fun and enjoyable, and promote fair play	
Always give enthusiastic and constructive feedback	
Treat everyone equally and with respect and dignity	
Build balanced relationships based on mutual trust	
Empower children to make their own decisions	
Be an excellent role model – take care of your appearance	

Good Practice Tool Box	Action Points
Work in an open environment – avoid closed, unobserved situations	
Listen to children and invite their opinion of your coaching	
Keep up to date with technical skills, insurance and qualifications	
Acknowledge the diverse roles that sport science can contribute towards the coaching process	
Observe all national governing body guidelines on manual support of children and explain them to children and their parents/carers	
Involve parents/carers in the supervision of children	
Carry out risk assessments and complete appropriate paperwork	
Keep accurate and up-to-date records	
Plan ahead for tournaments and competitions	
Ensure adequate staffing for away events in line with club, national governing body and local authority guidelines	

Now turn over.

Good Practice Tool Box	Action Points
Review transport arrangements for staff and performers	
Check all kit and equipment frequently for signs of wear and tear	
Identify when to have a break from coaching responsibilities	
Practice emergency situations (eg fire, injury)	
Add any extra examples of good practice that you can think of in the space provided below:	

Recognising Poor Practice

As well as adopting and promoting good practice, it is also important to recognise examples of poor practice (ie actions that fail to comply with the key principles of good practice and child protection). These could include:

- rough, physical and/or sexually provocative games
- inappropriate touching
- children using inappropriate language without being challenged
- children being reduced to tears as a form of control
- the use of sexually suggestive comments, even in jest
- allegations made by a child going unchallenged.

This list is not exhaustive and you may be able to identify additional examples. In all cases, poor practice must be challenged and attempts made to rectify the situation.

Use team meetings to discuss actual and potential examples of good and poor practice. This will help to foster an open and positive sporting environment.

Demonstrating Good Practice

You may think that you already have a responsible attitude towards your role as a coach. This may well be the case, but what evidence do you have of this? The following activity asks you to evaluate and reflect on specific coaching scenarios in which you would need to demonstrate responsible and professional practice.

ACTIVITY 9

Read through each of the following scenarios. In the spaces provided, note down:

a) any views or concerns you may have

b) a possible solution to the situation.

1 A gifted young performer in an U14 squad requests individual, one-to-one coaching even though they are part of a group.

a Your views/concerns:

b Possible solution:

2 Some children whom you coach ask to visit your house to see your collection of sports medals and trophies, and to borrow some training manuals.

a Your views/concerns:

b Possible solution:

3 You are asked to attend a training weekend where, for supervisory purposes, you are allocated a sleeping area with a group of children.

a Your views/concerns:

b Possible solution:

4 A new coach uses inappropriate language which the children repeat, making fun of other groups in a loud, suggestive manner.

a Your views/concerns:

b Possible solution:

Continued ...

5 You are asked to coach a young adult with special needs, but are not given time to discuss her specific personal requirements, neither with the young adult herself nor her carer.

a Your views/concerns:

b Possible solution:

6 A child in your care receives a bang to his head. He appears to be fine and you forget to inform his parents and omit to complete an accident report.

a Your views/concerns:

b Possible solution:

7 During a coaching session, a young performer begins to suggest that they really like you and would like to meet you for a coffee.

a Your views/concerns:

b Possible solution:

8 You are asked to take a squad to an away fixture by yourself.

a Your views/concerns:

b Possible solution:

Now turn over.

Feedback

All the scenarios in this activity are examples of situations in which things are not quite right and where a common-sense approach is required. As a coach, it is important to demonstrate exemplary behaviour at all times in order to protect yourself from false allegations. This involves:

- *putting the welfare of your performers first*
- *treating everyone equally*
- *working in an open environment*
- *maintaining a safe distance from performers and refraining from intimacy (this includes avoiding sharing a room)*
- *avoiding spending time alone with children away from others – never offer a child a lift home if this would mean being alone with the child*
- *building coaching relationships based on trust*
- *promoting fair play*
- *being an excellent role model*
- *involving parents or carers*
- *giving enthusiastic feedback and avoiding negative criticism.*

NB This list is not exhaustive and is by no means definitive.

1.5 Summary

In this first section, you have been introduced to four key principles relating to good coaching practice:

- Rights
- Relationships
- Responsibilities: personal standards
- Responsibilities: professional standards.

You have also considered these principles in the context of coaching children and should now understand the crucial role you play in the development of sport and in the lives of the children you coach.

You should also have begun to think about the issues arising from the key principles and the action required to address them. Good practice involves ensuring that these actions result in a professional approach to coaching where there is evidence of honesty, integrity and competence. The aim is to provide sporting opportunities for children – for fun as well as for achievement – within a safe and secure environment.

For further information relating to some of the issues explored in this section, the following **scUK** leaflets are particularly recommended[1]:

- *Code of Conduct for Sports Coaches* (2001)
- *Safe and Sound* (updated 2001).

In the next section you will start to address the issues surrounding child abuse in general and, in particular, poor practice in sport. Examine your own feelings as you work through it. Initially, you may believe it has nothing to do with you because you think child abuse does not happen in your sport. Alternatively, you may accept that it occurs, but feel this material is irrelevant because it does not apply to your own behaviour (or that of your peer group coaches). For some of you, the material may create a strong emotional reaction, perhaps because you have been abused yourself, know someone who has, or have concerns about a particular child or adult with whom you sometimes work. Whatever your initial feelings, you will not be alone. You may also find that your attitude or feelings change as you work through the pack.

1 Both leaflets are available from Coachwise Ltd (Tel 0113-231 1310 or visit www.1st4sport.com).

Section Two

Understanding and Identifying Signs of Child Abuse

2.0 Introduction

All those directly or indirectly involved with children's sport have a responsibility to:

- explore their own values and attitudes in relation to child abuse
- be able to recognise signs and indicators of child abuse.

Even for those experienced in working with child abuse, it is not always easy to recognise situations where abuse has already taken place or may potentially occur. As a coach, you are not expected to be an expert, but you do have a responsibility to act if you have any concerns about the behaviour of an adult or a child towards another child.

In this section, you will be given the opportunity to explore what child abuse is and to consider your own feelings, beliefs and values towards it. Through the use of case studies, you will begin to differentiate categories of abuse and will then be encouraged to start to recognise the signs and indicators. Although quite factual, this section is intended to stimulate both thought and discussion. By the end of the section, you should be able to:

- consider your own beliefs and preconceived ideas about child abuse
- describe the different categories of child abuse
- describe the effects of abuse
- describe the incidence of abuse and identify those children most at risk
- identify the signs and symptoms of child abuse in sports situations.

2.1 What Constitutes Child Abuse?

The term *child abuse* is used to describe all the ways in which children are harmed, usually by adults and often by those they know and trust. It refers to the damage that has been, or may be, done to a child's physical or mental health. This damage may occur at home, at school or even within a sports environment. An adult may abuse a child both by inflicting harm and by failing to prevent harm. Alternatively, a child may abuse another child – indeed, there is growing evidence to suggest that peer abuse is an increasing concern for young people.

The following activity is designed to begin to address your own feelings when faced with an incident of potential child abuse.

Action Plus

ACTIVITY 10

Read through the following scenario:

At the end of a coaching session, you dismiss your group of children and escort them to the changing area. Outside the changing rooms, you notice several parents waiting to collect their children and go across to join them. As the children reappear from the changing rooms, you notice one mum looking cross as her son George trails various items of clothing across the floor, dropping a pile of clothes at her feet. George's mum has parked on a double yellow line and can see a traffic warden approaching.

George struggles to put his kit in his bag and can't find one of his trainers. His mum pushes him back quite harshly in the direction of the changing rooms and shouts at him to hurry up. You notice there are two other children in George's mum's car, both of whom appear to be crying.

When George finally emerges from the changing rooms with his missing trainer, his mum is having a lively discussion with the traffic warden who, despite her pleas, gives her a parking ticket. George attempts to get in the car, but is stopped by his mum who continues to shout and blames him for the parking fine. The last you see is George rubbing his head as he fumbles with his seat belt.

Now jot down your initial feelings:

Now turn over.

Feedback

A whole range of emotions may be experienced when faced with possible child abuse. Many people feel emotions such as anger, shock and dismay, perhaps followed by feelings of sorrow, sadness or sympathy. These feelings are very natural and important in order to continue to be sensitive to children's experience of abuse.

Try to identify what you understand by the term abuse by assessing the situations in the following activity.

ACTIVITY 11

Consider which of the following behaviours between children and adults are acceptable and which are not (and may therefore constitute abuse). Circle one of the answers for each example[1].

1	A four-year-old being left alone for half an hour.	Not acceptable / acceptable
2	A twelve-year-old child being left alone in the house for the evening.	Not acceptable / acceptable
3	A five-year-old girl sent to school in January wearing a thin cotton dress and summer jacket.	Not acceptable / acceptable
4	A thirteen-year-old boy going without lunch and dinner.	Not acceptable / acceptable
5	An instructor taking a group hill walking without adequate clothing.	Not acceptable / acceptable
6	A father smacking his twelve-year-old daughter because she was two hours late getting home.	Not acceptable / acceptable
7	An organisation whose requirements for a particular competition cause the performer to make abnormal changes to his or her body composition/shape.	Not acceptable / acceptable
8	A father bathing his eleven-year-old daughter.	Not acceptable / acceptable
9	A mother bathing her ten-year-old son.	Not acceptable / acceptable

1 Some of these questions were adapted from an original exercise developed by the Open University in *Child Abuse and Neglect: An Introduction* (1989).

10	A female babysitter bathing a ten-year-old boy who is physically disabled.	Not acceptable / acceptable
11	A male coach entering the girls' changing room to talk before the competition.	Not acceptable / acceptable
12	A male coach physically supporting a young female gymnast during a tumbling routine.	Not acceptable / acceptable
13	A coach having sexual intercourse with one of his sixteen-year-old athletes.	Not acceptable / acceptable
14	A male coach expressing his delight following good performance by slapping the buttocks of one of his young female athletes.	Not acceptable / acceptable
15	A parent having sexual intercourse with his or her child.	Not acceptable / acceptable
16	A female coach working alone with a squad of male athletes.	Not acceptable / acceptable
17	Parents making their sixteen-year-old son/daughter help out in the family shop every night and each weekend rather than being allowed to socialise with his/her peer group.	Not acceptable / acceptable
18	Parents constantly taunting their twelve-year-old son who hates sport and enjoys ballroom dancing.	Not acceptable / acceptable
19	A teacher who regularly undermines the efforts of a fifteen-year-old girl and publicly reports all the errors she makes with her homework.	Not acceptable / acceptable
20	A coach driving an eight-year-old to exhaustion and tears during training.	Not acceptable / acceptable
21	A player calling another player names.	Not acceptable / acceptable
22	Initiation ceremonies within sports teams.	Not acceptable / acceptable

Now turn over.

Feedback

You may have found that some of the examples were quite easy to respond to (eg a parent having sexual intercourse with their child is clearly illegal, unacceptable and constitutes abusive behaviour). Some are also covered by legislation – for example, the age of consent for sexual intercourse is 16 in England, Wales, Ireland and Scotland.

You will probably have found others more difficult and found yourself saying 'It would depend on ...' or 'I would need to know more about ...'. Some of these would not constitute child abuse (eg because of the age of the performer) nor would they contravene legislation. However, the issues they raise could be considered as part of an ethical code of practice for coaches and others involved in children's sport.

Remember!

Defining child abuse is made more difficult because of each person's different values and ideas about what constitutes child abuse. Most of the statements on pages 42 to 43 do not provide enough information for you to determine whether the behaviour constitutes neglect or abuse. However, as a coach, it is **not your responsibility to decide**. Your role is to be aware of possible indicators of abuse in order to inform others appropriately.

2.2 Truths and Myths

Having explored your feelings a little more fully, assess your current knowledge about child abuse and neglect by answering the questions in the next activity.

ACTIVITY 12

A number of commonly held views are stated below. Decide whether each is true or false:

1	Children are abused mostly by strangers.	True / False
2	It is only men who sexually abuse children.	True / False
3	Disabled children are less likely to be victims of abuse.	True / False
4	Girls are much more likely to be abused than boys.	True / False
5	It is more acceptable in some cultures for children to be abused.	True / False
6	If social services are involved, children are usually removed from their homes.	True / False
7	Children are resilient and therefore recover quickly from abuse.	True / False
8	Children under the age of five are more likely to be abused than older children.	True / False
9	More children are abused now than 20 years ago.	True / False
10	Children often lie about abuse.	True / False
11	There is widespread reported occurrence of abuse in sport.	True / False
12	Coaches have many opportunities to abuse children emotionally as well as physically.	True / False

Now turn over.

Feedback

1 **False**
Most children who are affected by abuse are abused by adults they know and trust.

2 **False**
Women also sexually abuse children, although far less than men. In figures for 1998, approximately 5% to 10% of the perpetrators of sexual abuse on children were women[1].

3 **False**
Disabled children are more vulnerable to abuse. They are more dependent on intimate care and sometimes less able to tell anyone or run away from abusive situations.

4 **False**
In 2000, NSPCC figures showed that, in general, the ratios were roughly equal. However, as the following table shows, in the case of ***serious sexual abuse overall****, girls are more likely to be abused than boys*[2]*:*

Table 1: Incidence of child abuse among under 18s in 2000

Type of Abuse	% of All Boys Under 18 Who Suffered this Type of Abuse in 2000	% of All Girls Under 18 Who Suffered this Type of Abuse in 2000
Serious absence of supervision	6	4
Sexual abuse by parents	1	1
Sexual abuse overall	7	16
Serious physical abuse	6	8

5 **False**
Child abuse is unacceptable in all cultures.

1 and 2 Figures taken from the NSPCC report *Child Maltreatment in the United Kingdom: A Study of the Prevalence of Child Abuse and Neglect* (2000).

6 **False**
Social services will only remove children when there is a risk of significant harm and if the child is in real danger of further abuse. Social services are there to work in partnership with parents or carers, and to offer as much support as possible. In 1995, the Department of Health estimated that around 160,000 children were referred to social services departments by all sources because of child protection concerns, and that 96% of those remained in the family home.

7 **False**
If untreated, the effects of abuse on children can be devastating and continue into adulthood.

8 **True**
In March 2001, social services child protection registers for England showed that:

- *40% of children at risk of abuse were less than five years old*
- *30% of children at risk of abuse were five to nine years old*
- *27% of children at risk of abuse were ten to fifteen years old*
- *2% of children at risk of abuse were aged sixteen and over*[1].

9 **False**
More incidents of child abuse are now reported than 20 years ago because of greater public awareness. However, more adults are now telling others about abuse that occurred during their childhood.

10 **False**
Children rarely lie about abuse. Very often they have been threatened that something bad will happen if they tell, which makes it vital that children are listened to and taken seriously.

11 **True**
A number of cases of sexual, physical or emotional abuse, bullying and neglect in sport have been reported in the media in recent years.

12 **True**
Some sports situations lend themselves to potential opportunities for emotional abuse to children (eg from the parents whose overwhelming ambition for their child exceeds the aspirations and potential of the child; the coach whose excessive criticism destroys the feelings of confidence and self-worth of the child).

Activities 11 and 12 helped you consider some of your own beliefs and preconceived ideas about child abuse. Unless these are explored, there is a danger that your judgement may be clouded or prejudiced. It is therefore important to be open-minded at all times. Having explored your beliefs and preconceived ideas, you will now be more receptive to the following information about categories and signs of abuse.

---

1 Figures taken from the Department of Health report *National Statistics* (2001) (see www.doh.gov.uk/public/cpr2001.htm for further details).

2.3 Categories of Abuse

Child abuse can take many forms, but can be broadly separated into five main categories:

- Neglect
- Physical abuse
- Sexual abuse
- Emotional abuse
- Bullying and harassment.

Neglect

Neglect occurs when adults fail to meet a child's basic physical and/or psychological needs, and is likely to result in the serious impairment of the child's health or development. Examples of neglect include:

- failing to provide adequate food, shelter and clothing
- constantly leaving children alone or unsupervised
- failing to protect a child from physical harm or danger
- failing to ensure access to appropriate medical care or treatment
- refusing to give children affection and attention.

Examples in sport

Neglect in a sport situation could include a coach failing to ensure that children are safe and comfortable, or exposing them to undue cold or to unnecessary risk of injury.

ACTIVITY 13

In the left-hand column of the table below, list situations in which neglect could occur in your sport. In the right-hand column, identify examples of good practice, which you undertake to ensure the safety of the children you coach.

Potential Examples of Neglect	Examples of Good Practice

Physical Abuse

Physical abuse occurs when someone physically hurts or injures a child by hitting, shaking, throwing, poisoning, burning or scalding, biting, suffocating, drowning, or otherwise causing deliberate physical harm to them. Giving children inappropriate drugs or alcohol also constitutes physical abuse.

Examples in sport

Physical abuse in a sport situation may be deemed to occur if the nature and intensity of training and competition exceeds the capacity of the child's immature and growing body. This includes instances where drugs are used to delay puberty, to control diet or to enhance performance.

Action Plus

ACTIVITY 14

In the space provided below, note down questions that you could ask to identify any concerns about physical issues relating to your sport and the children you coach. An example has been given to start you off.

Example
Should I encourage children to consume high-energy drinks or tablets prior to a race during a competition?

Sexual Abuse

Sexual abuse occurs when adults or other children (both male and female) use children to meet their own sexual needs. This could include full sexual intercourse, masturbation, oral sex, anal intercourse or fondling. Showing children pornographic material (eg books, videos, pictures) also constitutes sexual abuse.

Examples in sport

There are situations within all sports in which the potential for this form of abuse exists:

- In some sports, physical contact between the coach and the child is essential for safety reasons (eg the coach supporting a gymnast on a piece of equipment) and formal guidelines should exist. However, the absence of such guidelines, or the failure on the part of the coach to follow them, could create situations in which sexual abuse could go unnoticed.
- Alternatively, failure on the part of the coach to explain the need for physical contact at the outset with parents/carers and children, may result in concerns that sexual abuse is taking place.
- There is evidence that some people have used sporting events as an opportunity to take inappropriate photographs or videos of young and disabled sportspeople in vulnerable positions.

sports coach UK

ACTIVITY 15

In the space provided below, record specific guidelines relating to physical contact in your sport. If you are not sure, contact your national governing body for advice and guidance.

Emotional Abuse

Children who have suffered neglect, physical or sexual abuse will also have suffered some level of emotional abuse. This is the emotional ill treatment of a child resulting in severe and persistent adverse effects on his or her emotional development. Children of all ages can be emotionally abused in a number of ways, such as through:

- imposing developmentally inappropriate expectations on them
- making them feel worthless, unloved, inadequate or valued only insofar as they meet the needs of another person
- making them feel frightened or in danger
- shouting at, threatening or taunting them
- overprotecting them or, conversely, failing to give them the love and affection they need.

Examples in sport

Emotional abuse may occur in sport if children are subjected to constant criticism, name-calling, sarcasm, bullying, racism or unrealistic pressure to consistently perform to high expectations. In some cases, this may come from parents and coaches.

Situations could also arise in which the media, internet, photographs or even a club notice board are used to inflict emotional abuse which could go unnoticed until it becomes a real problem. Personal information in the wrong hands can be very upsetting for any performer.

As a result of emotional abuse, children may feel nervous, lack confidence and self-worth, and learn to dislike any form of activity. It is up to the coach to lead by example and to ensure that incidents of emotional abuse are handled with care and sensitivity, so that the situation is controlled and not made worse.

ACTIVITY 16

In the diagram provided below, record the groups of people who could be responsible for subjecting a child to emotional abuse in your sport – you may wish to discuss these with other coaches first. An example has been given to start you off.

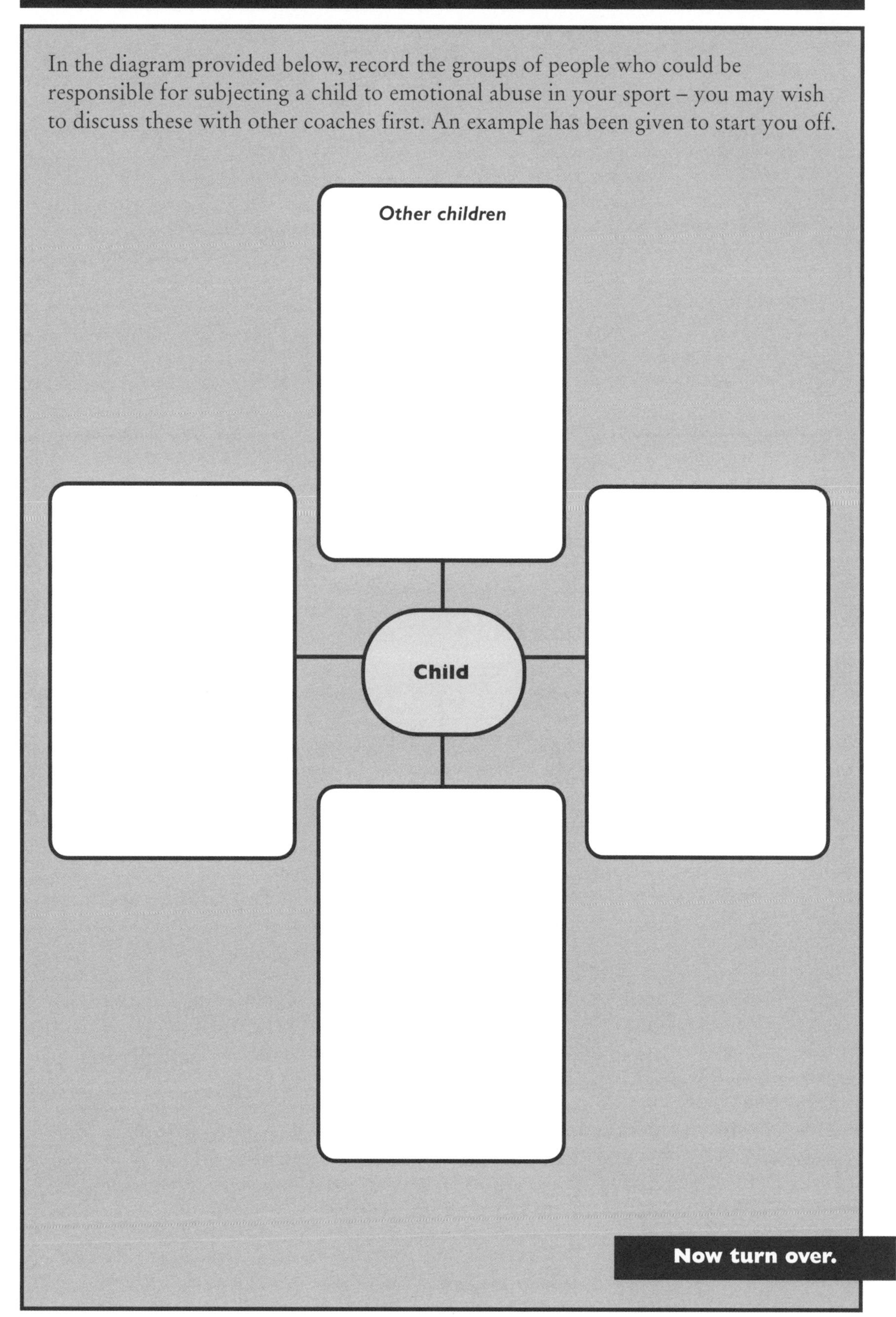

Now turn over.

Feedback

The diagram below shows examples of people who could be responsible for subjecting a child to emotional abuse in your sport. It also indicates some of the questions you should ask yourself to try and identify any situations in which there may be cause for concern.

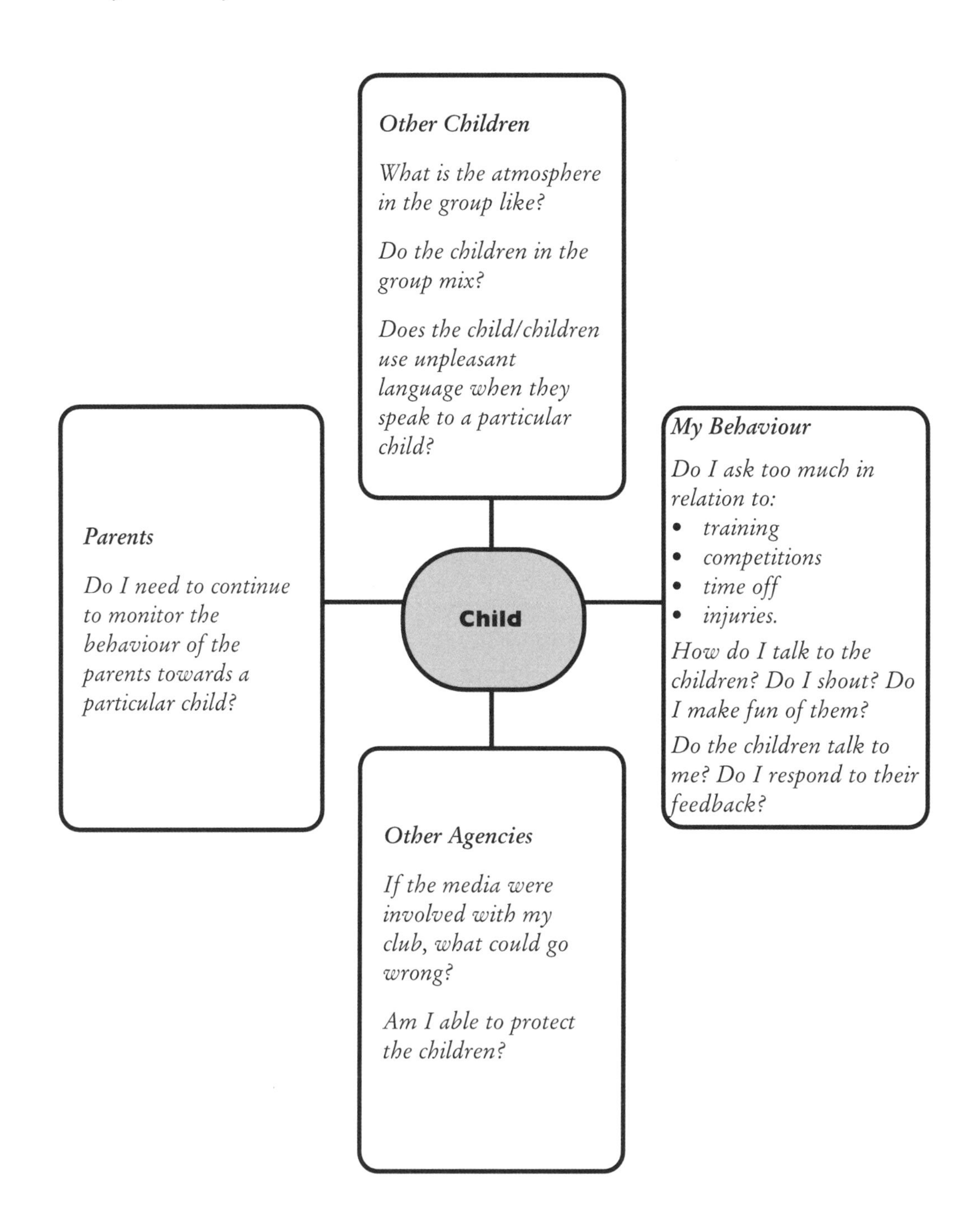

Bullying and Harassment

Bullying is deliberately hurtful behaviour, usually repeated over a period of time, where it is difficult for those bullied to defend themselves. It can be verbal, written or physical and can include actions such as physical assaults, name-calling, sarcasm, racist taunts, threats, gestures, unwanted physical contact, graffiti, stealing or hiding personal items. Bullying can even occur via the Internet.

Although anyone can be the target of bullying, victims are typically shy, sensitive or insecure. Sometimes they are singled out for physical reasons (eg being overweight or smaller than everyone else, having a disability, belonging to a different race, faith or culture).

In November 2000, the NSPCC published the results of major research[1] carried out to explore the childhood experience of young people in the UK, including their experience of abuse and neglect. The survey found that:

- 43% of the young people questioned identified bullying or being discriminated against by other children as the most common source of distress or misery
- bullying occurred mostly because of personal characteristics such as size, dress, race or manner of speech
- name-calling and verbal abuse were the most common forms of bullying
- 14–15% of the young people questioned were physically attacked
- many reported having had their property stolen or damaged.

The report concludes that for many children, the wider world of school, friends and community contains threats of bullying and discrimination and, for girls in particular, sexual harassment and violence.

The effects of bullying may be invisible, but can leave lasting emotional scars. The bully is not always obvious to others and the victim often keeps quiet.

Harassment is closely associated with aspects of bullying and occurs when an individual feels that they are subject to behaviour from others that is unacceptable to them. Such behaviour could include simple name-calling or an action that is designed to annoy, upset or worry another child. In some cases, it may develop into an identifiable pattern of bullying; in other more subtle cases, it may take the form of random acts – again designed to upset others.

1 *Child Maltreatment in the United Kingdom: A Study of the Prevalence of Child Abuse and Neglect* (2000)

Examples in sport

The competitive nature of sport makes it an ideal environment for the bully. This could be:

- a parent who pushes his or her child too hard
- a coach who shouts at, or humiliates, children
- children who actively seek to make sport a difficult or unhappy experience for others.

Although bullying often takes place in schools, it can and does occur wherever there is the opportunity for children to meet (eg changing rooms, practice and social areas in sports centres, during journeys to and from sports activities). The bully is not selective in the location, but is always careful about who else may be able to observe what is said or done. The damage inflicted by bullying is frequently underestimated. It can cause considerable distress to some children to the extent that they may stop participating in sport altogether.

Although it may be difficult for you to anticipate when your actions could provide further opportunities for the bully, you have a responsibility to ensure that sport is a positive experience for all children. Carefully observe the children you coach to evaluate whether they are being included in activities by other children and whether they have the confidence to voice any doubts they may have. It is easy to tell if children are unhappy – you cannot get the best out of them if they are hurting emotionally.

ACTIVITY 17

1. Read through the following scenarios and decide whether they are examples of how children avoid being bullied. Indicate your response in the middle column of the table.
2. Try to work out why their behaviour is not quite what you would expect. Note your ideas in the right-hand column of the table.

Scenario	Yes/No	Reasons
1 You notice that a member of a team that you coach will not get changed at the same time as everyone else. She always arrives in her kit and stays late to clear up the equipment or just to chat, so that by the time she goes into the changing rooms, everyone else is leaving. She declines the offer of a free fitness test and fails to attend a club outing to the local swimming pool. When you think about it, you realise that this child always remains fully covered for every activity and is often on her own.		
2 You hear that a new member of your coaching group is from another area of the town and that the other team members do not like him. Teams for today's game were decided last week, so the newcomer has to wait for an opportunity to join in. You decide to ask him to help referee the game and tell him he will be able to play later on. However, during the first few minutes of play, he blows the whistle and makes a controversial decision. This upsets the team members and, when the newcomer joins the team, he is left out of play. The rest of the team members pass the ball among themselves and seem to call the newcomer names. You notice that after the session, the team members are quiet and the atmosphere is very icy. The newcomer changes quickly and leaves.		
3 You ask a group you coach to work with an older mixed team for training purposes. Most of the team members feel that this is an excellent idea, but some members of the group look worried. The older team contains skilled, technical players. They are bigger, heavier and have a reputation for playing very hard.		

Now turn over.

Feedback

Scenario 1
Some children have a strong desire to maintain privacy. In this case, the child has a skin condition that other children will ask about if they see it and will probably make fun of. By avoiding getting changed in public, this child ensures that the condition remains a secret and maintains the appearance that she is the same as everyone else.

Scenario 2
This scenario is very common. There are several issues here: children often have problems with children from areas other than their own; they like to stick with the friendship groups they have formed already; they will not readily accept changes to teams. Placing the newcomer in a position of authority as a referee causes several further problems. He not only has to demonstrate his rule knowledge and be efficient, but also has to show which team he would prefer to be associated with. Being new is difficult enough without being made to stand out as well. This situation could get worse before it gets better.

Scenario 3
This scenario exposes players to the unknown. Straight away, several children will feel inadequate and reluctant to play with older players because they don't want to look silly. Others, however, simply may not want to play a mixed game – mixing teams is never easy.

2.4 Effects of Abuse

The effects of child abuse can be devastating, especially if children are left unprotected or do not have access to people who can help them cope with abuse.

As a result of abuse, children may:

- die – clearly the most serious effect
- suffer pain and distress
- develop behavioural difficulties, such as becoming angry and aggressive
- experience a developmental delay (physically, emotionally and mentally)
- experience school-related problems (eg loss of concentration, even refusing to go to school altogether)
- develop low self-esteem
- suffer depression or inflict self-harm, sometimes leading to suicide attempts
- become withdrawn or introverted
- suffer temporary or even permanent injury.

Adult survivors of child abuse typically say that their childhood experiences have made them feel guilty and worthless. They may have blamed themselves for what happened which in turn led to anxiety, depression and sometimes difficulty in forming or maintaining relationships. If help is not provided, the behaviour displayed by children who have been abused may persist into adult life and can sometimes lead to abusive relationships with their own children or with other adults.

2.5 Incidence of Abuse

How many children are abused?

The following table is taken from *Children and Young People on Child Protection Registers* by the Department of Health (2000). The child protection register indicates children who have been abused or are at serious risk of abuse.

Table 2: Estimates of national incidence of child abuse per year (includes figures for England, Northern Ireland and Wales)

Category of Abuse	1998	1999	2000
Neglect alone	8209	12,562	12,426
Physical injury alone	5410	7494	6791
Sexual abuse alone	5930	5376	4301
Emotional abuse alone	217	6086	6209
Neglect, physical and sexual abuse	1892	216	313
Neglect and physical injury	872	1926	2056
Neglect and sexual abuse	772	888	877
Physical injury and sexual abuse	300	778	780
Categories not recommended by *Working Together*[1]	200	500	300
No category available	11,634	200	100
Total	35,436	36,026	34,153

These figures clearly demonstrate an increase in the incidence of abuse between 1998 and 2000. As yet, no figures relating specifically to sport are available. However, the fact that there are known cases of abuse in sport is evidence enough. Every possible measure should therefore be taken to ensure that sport is a safe experience for children.

1 *Working Together to Safeguard Children* (1999)

Risks

Child abuse can happen to children of all ages, regardless of their gender, race, culture or background. What places children at risk of abuse?

Some children are perceived as being more vulnerable than others. Assessing the overall risk to a child is a very complex task, undertaken by child protection professionals. This process takes account of many factors such as:

- high levels of stress
- previous violence in the family
- poor relationships between parents or carers
- the age of the child.

However, even when many of these factors exist, it does not necessarily mean that the child concerned will be abused.

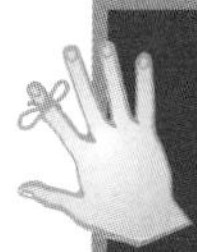

Remember!

There are certain categories of children who may be especially at risk for various reasons:

- Very young children, and those with a physical disability or learning difficulty, may be more vulnerable to abuse. They may also find it more difficult to tell people – either because of language difficulties or limited access to people they can trust.[1]
- Children from ethnic minorities who are being abused, and who may also be experiencing racial discrimination, may find it hard to tell someone because they feel doubly powerless.
- Children in a sport situation may be vulnerable because of the possible use of physical contact (eg through physical demonstration, supporting movements) or through the use of emotional blackmail (eg 'It's the only way you will reach the top levels').

1 Based on information from *The Abuse of Children and Adults with Disabilities* (1993)

To compound the problems, adults do not always hear or see the messages children give to indicate that they are being abused. This places children at further risk. Abused children may also behave in ways that adults find it difficult to cope with and which make them more vulnerable. However, recent research clearly indicates that children and adults can recover from the effects of abuse if they are believed, protected from further abuse and receive the help they need to overcome the experiences they have suffered[1].

Before moving on to the next section, you may wish to complete the following activity to check you have grasped the essential information.

Action Plus

1 Further information is available on the NSPCC website (www.nspcc.org.uk).

ACTIVITY 18

1 List the main categories of child abuse and give a brief explanation of each:

Category	Explanation

2 List the main effects of abuse on children:

3 List any factors that may increase the likelihood of risk:

Now turn over.

Feedback

1 *The main forms of child abuse are explained in the following table:*

Category	Explanation
Physical abuse	*This includes hitting, burning and biting; giving children alcohol, inappropriate drugs or poison; attempted suffocation or drowning; excessive or inappropriate training regimes; use of drugs to enhance performance or delay puberty.*
Neglect	*Failure to meet a child's basic needs (eg food, warm clothing); leaving children alone or unsupervised; failure to give love or affection.*
Emotional abuse	*Persistent lack of love and affection; children being constantly threatened or taunted; parents or coaches whose overwhelming ambition exceeds that of the child; persistent disregard of a child's effort or progress.*
Sexual abuse	*Where adults use children to meet their own sexual needs. This includes sexual intercourse, masturbation, oral sex, anal intercourse or fondling, as well as showing children pornographic videos or magazines, or taking photos of children for inappropriate use.*
Bullying	*It is now recognised that, in some cases of abuse, the abuser may not always be an adult, but could be a child. Bullying may be seen as deliberate, hurtful behaviour, usually repeated over a period of time, where it is difficult for those bullied to defend themselves.*

2 *The main effects of abuse on children are as follows:*

- *Children may die*
- *Pain and distress*
- *Behavioural difficulties, such as becoming angry and aggressive*
- *School-related problems*
- *Developmental delay – physically, emotionally and mentally*
- *Low self-esteem*
- *Depression, self-harm – sometimes leading to suicide*
- *Difficulty in forming relationships as adults*
- *Sometimes, if untreated, abusive relationships with own (or other) children*
- *Temporary or even permanent injury.*

3 *Factors that may increase the likelihood of risk:*

- *Young children who may have difficulty telling others.*
- *Disabled children who may have difficulty communicating or accessing people to tell.*
- *Children who are already experiencing some form of discrimination (eg racial harassment), because this is a further form of abuse.*
- *Poor relationship between children and parents/carers.*
- *High levels of stress.*
- *History of violence in the family.*

If you have had any difficulty with this activity, you may wish to re-read Sections 2.3, 2.4 and 2.5 before moving onto Section 2.6.

Action Plus

2.6 Identifying Signs of Abuse

Recognising abuse is not easy, even for individuals who are experienced in working with abuse. Often personal feelings of shock or anger can interfere with the recognition that abuse is taking place, and it is easy to deny that it is happening. This section is not designed to make you an expert, but to make you more alert to the signs of possible abuse in all five areas. By the end, you should be able to identify the possible signs and indicators of each type of abuse – neglect, physical, sexual, emotional and bullying or harassment. Start by tackling the next activity.

Action Plus

ACTIVITY 19

Jot down any signs or indicators that would make you concerned that a child is being abused. An example has been given to start you off.

Example
Unexplained injuries or bruising

Now turn over.

Feedback

The list you have compiled may cover some or all of the following indicators:

- *Unexplained bruising or injuries*
- *Sexually explicit actions or language*
- *Changes in behaviour or mood*
- *Something a child has said*
- *A change observed over a long period of time (eg weight loss, increasingly dirty or unkempt).*

All these factors are important and children may often suffer from more than one form of abuse. For example, a child who is repeatedly smacked for minor misdemeanours may also experience emotional abuse because they feel frightened, anxious or worthless.

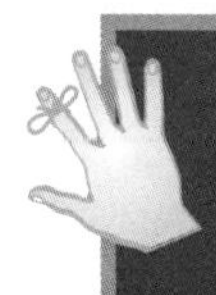

Remember!

*Evidence of a **combination or repetition of signs over time** should alert you to possible problems, not just one bruise.*

Neglect

Because neglect is where adults fail to meet a child's basic physical and/or psychological needs, it is likely to result in the serious impairment of the child's health or development. It can go unnoticed for a long time, yet have lasting and very damaging effects on children. Children who do not receive adequate food or physical care will often develop and mature more slowly, while those who are left alone, unsupervised or unoccupied will often find it difficult to make friends or socialise adequately. It is important to look for both physical and emotional indicators.

Remember!

Physical indicators of neglect include:

- constant hunger, sometimes stealing food from other children
- an unkempt state (frequently dirty or smelly)
- loss of weight or being constantly underweight
- inappropriate dress.

Behavioural indicators of neglect include:

- being tired all the time
- frequently being late for school or not going to school at all
- failing to attend hospital or medical appointments
- having few friends
- being left alone or unsupervised on a regular basis.

ACTIVITY 20

Read John's story, then answer the questions provided.

John is fourteen years of age and uses a wheelchair. He is cared for by his dad, as his mum died over a year ago. He has been learning basketball over the past three years and is delighted to have been chosen to participate in an international tour in six months' time. This clearly involves a good deal of planning and a number of meetings.

John does not attend the first two meetings. He says his dad is unable to bring him. For the second two meetings, you offer to collect John and return him home in the evenings at about 10pm. You agree this with his dad and let other coaches in your club know about the arrangement. In this case, it is difficult to say no to requests for transport, even though you are not really comfortable with the situation. On both occasions, there is no-one at home and the house is cold and dark. John has not eaten since lunchtime. You offer to make John a cup of tea and, on going to the cupboard, find there is very little food. John does not know where his dad is; he seems to accept the fact that he may not return until much later, and says he is quite often left alone, sometimes all night. John doesn't seem to mind, for he says he can get himself to bed and his dad is usually there in the mornings.

1 As John feels quite happy about his dad not being there, do you feel it is acceptable for him to be alone?

2 What do you think you might do in this situation?

Now turn over.

Feedback

This is a very difficult situation. It is certainly unacceptable for any young person to be left alone overnight, even if quite mature. John may have additional needs – for example, if there was a fire in the house, he would be at increased risk because he may not be able to move as quickly as a non-disabled person. It is an additional concern that John does not know where his dad is, or when he will be back.

The fact that John is left on his own regularly is of concern. A lack of heating is particularly worrying as John is in a wheelchair and has limited mobility.

The lack of food is difficult to judge. Does this happen all the time or is it unusual? His dad may be due to buy food. If it is a regular occurrence, however, John's basic needs are clearly not being met.

What happened?

Even though John did not mind being alone, the situation he was in is not acceptable. After a discussion with the club manager, and then with social services, John and his dad said they did not want anyone to interfere. John's dad had not really appreciated John's needs. He thought he was sufficiently responsible. He agreed not to leave John alone again for such long periods.

Physical Abuse

Most children will collect cuts and bruises in their daily life, and certainly through their involvement in sport.

ACTIVITY 21

1 Jot down the typical soft tissue injuries likely to be sustained in your sport:

2 Note any areas where you might expect abrasions and bruising from participation in your sport:

Now turn over.

Feedback

Minor cuts, bruises and soft tissue injuries (eg strains and tears) are quite common in some sports. The areas where bruising is most likely to occur are the bony parts of the body (eg elbows, knees, shins or forehead).

Remember!

You should be aware of children's injuries or bruising which can only be caused non-accidentally. These will often be part of a recurring pattern, sometimes appearing regularly (eg after a weekend). An important indicator of physical abuse is where bruises or injuries are:

- unexplained
- untreated
- inadequately treated (or where there are delays to treatment)
- on parts of the body where accidental injuries are unlikely (eg on the cheeks or thighs).

Bruising may be more or less noticeable on children with different skin tones or from different racial groups. You need to be alert to the following **physical indicators**:

- Unexplained bruising, marks or injuries on any part of the body
- Bruises that reflect hand marks or fingertips (from slapping, grabbing, pinching)
- Cigarette burns
- Bite marks
- Broken bones (particularly if the child is under two years old)
- Scalds.

Physical abuse may not always be apparent from bruises, fractures or physical signs. **Behavioural indicators**, particularly when there are changes in behaviour, can also indicate that abuse is happening. This might be evident in the following behaviours:

- Fear of parents being contacted
- Aggressive behaviour or severe temper outbursts
- Running away
- Fear of going home (eg after training sessions)
- Flinching when approached or touched
- Reluctance to get changed for sport
- Covering arms and legs even when hot (eg during hard physical activity or in hot weather)
- Depression
- Withdrawn behaviour.

ACTIVITY 22

Read Mary's story, then answer the questions provided.

Mary Carter is six years of age. She has come to swimming lessons during the summer holidays with her elder brother Peter, who is ten. Mary and Peter's family is well known in the local area; their father is a bank manager at the local branch and their mother is a senior manager at a local computer company. Mary's mother, Pamela, works long hours and is often away on business. However, Mary and Peter are normally happy, lively and outgoing children.

Yesterday, Mrs Carter came to collect Mary and Peter from the leisure centre but was clearly in a rush. Mary had not finished changing and Mrs Carter bundled her roughly out of the centre into the car. Today, Mary arrives at the pool in a distressed state. During the lesson, Catherine, Mary's coach, notices that she has five straight red marks on the back of her thigh.

1 Do you think Catherine should be concerned about Mary? If so, why?

2 What do you think are the causes of the marks on Mary's leg?

3 Are there any other concerns you have about this situation?

Now turn over.

Feedback

There are a number of reasons why Catherine should be concerned:

- *The back of the thigh is an unusual place for marks to appear. It would be improbable that these marks would be caused accidentally. Straight red marks could indicate hand mark bruising, or having been hit with another straight implement.*
- *Mrs Carter's behaviour towards Mary may suggest that there is a degree of stress in the family. Mary's distress could be for a number of reasons but it could be clearly linked to what is going on at home. What is important is the change in Mary's usual behaviour.*

What happened?

In the end, Catherine was able to talk gently to Mary about why she was upset. Mrs Carter had lost her temper and slapped Mary hard, leaving marks. Catherine reported her concerns to the sports centre manager, who knew Mary's parents. He agreed to talk to Mrs Carter. It transpired that Mr and Mrs Carter had decided to separate and had been under extreme stress in this situation. Mrs Carter was initially very angry and upset but subsequently agreed to let the manager phone social services to arrange some help for the family. Social services were able to work with all the family members for a short period of time to help alleviate the stress.

ACTIVITY 23

Jot down any other form of potential physical abuse that occurs or may occur in your sport:

Now turn over.

Feedback

In sports in which advantages are gained by delaying the onset of puberty (eg the potential strength/weight advantages of prepubescent female gymnasts), drugs and diet may be used to retard physical and sexual development. This may result in serious medical disorders such as anorexia or osteoporosis. In other sports where strength or power are key attributes (eg weight lifting), there is potential abuse from performance-enhancing drugs.

In any sport, there is also the potential for physical abuse from overuse injuries. Children should avoid training or competing when suffering from injury or before injury or illness rehabilitation has been fully completed.

Sexual Abuse

How will you know if a child is being sexually abused? Because physical signs are difficult to observe on a day-to-day, routine basis, a child's behaviour may be the only outward indicator of sexual abuse.

Children may tell you either directly or indirectly that they are being sexually abused. This will have taken enormous courage on their part because it is likely that they will have been threatened by the abuser about what will happen if they tell, and/or will be aware and very frightened of the potential consequences (eg the abuser going to prison). In all cases, children will tell you because they want the abuse to stop. Therefore, it is very important that you listen to them and take them seriously.

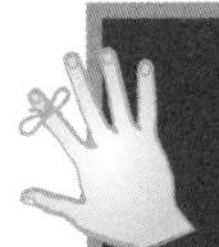

Remember!

There may be **physical indicators** of sexual abuse such as:

- pain or itching in the genital area
- bruising or bleeding near the genital area
- a sexually transmitted disease
- vaginal discharge or infection
- stomach pains
- discomfort when walking or sitting down
- pregnancy.

If you suspect or become aware of such indicators it is inappropriate for you to check them out yourself. In these circumstances, always refer the child to a medical expert.

The sort of **behavioural indicators** you may notice include:

- sudden or unexplained changes in behaviour (eg becoming aggressive or withdrawn)
- apparent fear of someone
- running away from home
- having nightmares
- sexual knowledge which is beyond the child's age or developmental level
- sexual drawings or language
- bed-wetting
- eating problems such as overeating or anorexia
- self-harm or mutilation, sometimes leading to suicide attempts
- children saying they have secrets they cannot tell anyone about
- substance or drug abuse
- a child suddenly having unexplained sources of money
- taking over a parental role at home and seeming beyond their age level
- children who are not allowed to have friends (particularly in adolescence)
- children acting in a sexually explicit way towards adults
- a child telling someone about the abuse.

Action Plus

ACTIVITY 24

Read the following story, then answer the questions provided.

Carole is a young woman, aged fourteen. She has learning difficulties, a developmental level of about eleven years and is partially hearing impaired, although she can lip-read. Carole is participating in outdoor activities as part of her school's curriculum. This means that she attends the outdoor centre every Wednesday afternoon. One afternoon there is an indoor lesson, covering the basic skills required for orienteering. During some individual time with Carole, she tells you that she does not like Tony, her mum's boyfriend. She does not say any more than this but later has a sudden outburst of temper, which is unusual. When Carole calms down it is nearly time to go home, although she seems very reluctant to go.

1 Would you start to have some concerns about Carole? If so, what would they be?

2 What do you think you might do at this stage?

Now turn over.

Feedback

1 *You may have mentioned the following issues of concern at this stage:*
- *The sudden outburst of temper, which is a change of behaviour.*
- *A reluctance to go home, linked to the dislike of one person.*
- *The particular vulnerabilities of disabled children in relation to abuse.*

2 *All these factors may indicate that Carole is being abused. At this stage it would be important to:*
- *ensure that time is given to Carole, preferably from a female coach, as children who have been abused by a man may prefer to talk to a woman and vice versa*
- *communicate with her sensitively and comment on the fact that she seems reluctant to go home*
- *ask if there is anything troubling her as she does not normally get upset*
- *share any concerns with a senior colleague.*

What happened?
After a long conversation about her worries, Carole eventually told the play worker that Tony had made her touch his genital area. The play worker spoke to the centre manager, who informed social services. The police and social services talked to Carole who told them what was happening. Tony denied the allegation but agreed to leave the family home. Social services continued to work with Carole and her mum, to help Carole overcome the traumatic effect of what happened.

Emotional Abuse

Emotional abuse is perhaps the most difficult of all forms of abuse to measure. Often, children who appear well cared for may be emotionally abused by being taunted, put down or belittled, or because they receive little or no love, affection or attention from their parents or carers. Coaches and others involved in performance sport should also consider the potential emotional abuse from excessive pressure during training regimes or in relation to competition.

Remember!

Physical indicators of emotional abuse may include:
- a failure to thrive or grow, particularly if the child puts on weight in other circumstances (eg in hospital or away from home)
- sudden speech disorders
- developmental delay, either in terms of physical or emotional progress.

Behavioural indicators may include:
- neurotic behaviour (eg hair twisting, rocking)
- being unable to play, unwilling to take part
- excessive fear of making mistakes
- sudden speech disorders
- self-harm or mutilation
- fear of parents being contacted.

ACTIVITY 25

Read the following story, then answer the questions provided.

Kea is twelve years old. She is Japanese and came to live in England with her parents two years ago. She is an excellent gymnast and a regular attendee at her local club. Both Kea's parents are supportive and encourage her gymnastics.

You are one of the coaches at the gymnastics club. Tom, one of your colleagues, usually coaches Kea. You have known Tom for years. He has a reputation for being one of the lads, and is always joking and teasing the young gymnasts, particularly the young women. Although you feel uncomfortable about this, the younger gymnasts seem eager to please Tom to gain his praise.

One Saturday morning, you notice that during a gymnastics exercise, Tom puts his arm around Kea's shoulders and then pats her bottom as she goes away. She makes a mistake during the exercise and Tom makes what you consider to be a racist comment. Later in the day, you hear him shouting at Kea, telling her she is rubbish and that there is no hope for her. Kea is clearly distressed by this but he ignores her. This is not the first time you have had concerns about Tom and you decide to challenge his behaviour. He puts you down, says you cannot take a joke and claims Kea enjoys all the attention.

1 What feelings does this raise for you?

2 Do you have concerns about the way Tom is behaving? If so, why?

3 What action do you think you might take?

Now turn over.

Feedback

1 *This is a very difficult situation. Although you may or may not think the way Tom is behaving is abusive, it is clearly unethical and reflects extremely poor practice. The feelings you have will probably range from anger at Tom's behaviour to concern for Kea. You may also feel guilty or frustrated because you have not done anything before now, yet confused because you have known Tom a long time and do not want to risk misconduct proceedings.*

2 *There are clearly concerns about Tom's behaviour. It is totally unacceptable to touch Kea in the way he did. Even what some may consider to be a friendly gesture (eg putting an arm around the shoulder) may be offensive to children and could be misconstrued. Likewise, offensive racist comments are in themselves abusive, as are comments which belittle children or make them feel worthless. These are behaviours, which initially may seem less serious than overt physical or sexual abuse. However, they are rarely one-off events and this kind of harassment and bullying of children is just as damaging in the long term.*

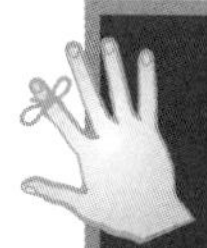

Remember!

In terms of good practice in the care of children, ***you should never:***

- *allow or engage in inappropriate touching of any form*
- *make sexually suggestive comments about or to a child, even in fun*
- *refer to a child's ethnicity, disability, gender or sexuality in a way which is derogatory*
- *allow children to use inappropriate language unchallenged*
- *engage in rough, physical or sexually provocative games or horseplay*
- *do things of a personal nature for children that they can do themselves. If children are very young or are disabled, these tasks should only be carried out with the consent of parents or carers. In an emergency situation, parents or carers should be informed. Discretion and sensitivity are important at all times.*[1]

1 Adapted from *Our Duty to Care* (1995) – this is a useful pack for voluntary organisations to protect children and staff. In addition, *Safe from Harm* (1993) offers a code of practice for safeguarding the welfare of children in voluntary organisations in England and Wales.

3 *Responding to concerns about a colleague's behaviour is very difficult, particularly if you know the person well, and the consequences of reporting allegations may have far-reaching effects. Nevertheless, poor practice cannot go unchallenged, for it may be part of a more serious problem of abuse, which places children at serious risk. It would be important to ensure that Kea is safe and that she is told she is not to blame. It would also be necessary to ensure that Kea and her parents know how to make a complaint. In addition, it would be important to challenge the behaviour with Tom. He may not realise the way he is behaving is offensive. If the behaviour continues or your concerns remain, you must refer the matter to a senior colleague or official at your club. It is their responsibility to contact social services and the police if it is a child protection issue, and/or instigate misconduct or disciplinary proceedings. If the concerns are about a senior colleague (or there is no senior colleague) you should refer the matter to the governing body child protection contact or to social services directly. You can also ring the NSPCC Helpline for advice (tel: 0808-800 5000).*

What happened?

In this situation, Tom's behaviour was reported to one person in charge at the gymnastics club. It transpired that this was not the first occasion on which concerns had been expressed about Tom's behaviour and the matter was taken seriously and acted upon immediately. Kea's parents were informed. The person in charge sought advice from the national governing body and Tom was suspended while misconduct proceedings were implemented.

The person in charge also referred the matter to the police and social services, and sought their advice. Tom was interviewed by the police, but no further action was taken. Under the misconduct proceedings, it was felt that, because Tom was not accepting responsibility for this or previous actions, and refused to acknowledge his behaviour, there was a probability that he would continue to behave in a way that was abusive to children. The club and the national governing body therefore did not reinstate him as a coach.

Bullying and Harassment

The damage inflicted by bullying and harassment is frequently underestimated. It can cause considerable distress to children, to the extent that it affects their health and development or, in extreme cases, causes them significant harm (including self-harm). There are a number of signs that may indicate that a child is being bullied:

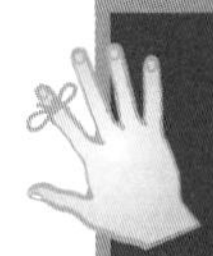

Remember!

Physical indicators may include:

- stomach-aches or headaches
- difficulty in sleeping
- bed-wetting
- scratching or bruising
- damaged clothes
- bingeing (eg on food, cigarettes or alcohol)
- a shortage of money
- frequent loss of possessions.

Behavioural indicators may include:

- reduced concentration
- becoming withdrawn or depressed
- being clingy
- being emotionally up and down (eg tearful)
- a reluctance to go to school/training
- a drop in performance in sport or at school.

2.7 Summary

In this section, you have had the chance to consider your own feelings about child protection issues and have been encouraged to consider specific situations.

You have also been asked to consider the different categories of abuse and should now be able to relate them to your own sport.

The indicators outlined in Section 2.6 are very important, but even if children display all of these signs, it does not necessarily mean they are being abused. **It is not your responsibility to decide**. However, it is your responsibility to **act if you suspect abuse**. Your observations could be the missing piece in a jigsaw of worries, which is already being pieced together by child protection professionals like social workers and the police. This is why it is vital that you are aware of all these signs and indicators, both in terms of what you see (ie physical signs) and in what you observe (ie behavioural signs).

Child abuse, particularly sexual abuse, can arouse strong emotions in those facing such a situation. It is important to understand these emotions and not to allow them to interfere with your judgement about what action to take.

In the last few activities in this section, you started to think about what you might do in certain situations. Section Three takes this a little further and considers what steps to take if you think a child is being abused.

Section Three

Taking Appropriate Action

3.0 Introduction

False allegations of abuse do occur, but they are rare. You should always take immediate action if a child says or indicates that he is being abused, or you have reason to suspect that this is the case. This may involve dealing with the child, his parent or carer, colleagues at your club/organisation, teachers, external agencies or the media.

In this section, you will be encouraged to consider how you should respond to a child for whom you have concerns, either as a result of a disclosure from the child, your own observations or the concerns of others. You will also see that, by developing procedures to both prevent and deal with such situations, it should be possible to provide a fun and safe sporting environment for children.

By the end of this section, you should be able to:

- describe how you would respond to a child who discloses evidence of abuse
- recognise the importance of your own observations in the detection of possible abuse
- identify the person(s) to whom you should report or share your concern
- deal with difficult situations involving allegations against parents/carers or other staff/volunteers
- deal with incidents of bullying
- describe the responsibilities of various agencies/organisations, including your club/organisation, national governing bodies, local authorities, social services and the police
- prepare yourself for the possibility of having to deal with suspected abuse in the future.

3.1 Dealing with Disclosures of Abuse

Children who are being abused will only tell people they trust and with whom they feel safe. Coaches very often share a close relationship with their performers and may therefore be the sort of person in whom a child might place her trust. Children want the abuse to stop. By listening and taking what a child is telling you seriously, you will already be helping to protect them.

It is useful to think in advance about how you might respond to this situation in such a way as to avoid putting yourself at risk. The following guidelines are included in most national governing body child protection policies and procedures, and it is strongly recommended that they are incorporated into the framework of your own club/organisation.

Timing and Location

Understandably, a child who has been abused may want to see you alone, away from others. She may therefore approach you at the end of a session when everyone is going home, or may arrive deliberately early at a time when she thinks you will not be busy. However, a disclosure is not just a quick chat, it will take time and usually has further consequences. Bear in mind that you may also need to attend to other children, check equipment or set up an activity – you cannot simply leave a session unattended. Therefore, try to arrange to speak to the child at an appropriate time.

Location is very important. Although it is important to respect the child's need for privacy, you also need to protect yourself against potential allegations. Do not listen to the child's disclosure in a completely private place – try to ensure that other members of staff are present or at least nearby.

Responding to the Child

It will have taken a great deal of courage for a child to tell you about abusive behaviour and it is crucial that you take this into consideration when responding to the child's disclosure. Following the guidance in the panel opposite will help you to act in an appropriate and responsible manner:

- Do not panic – react calmly so as not to frighten the child.
- Acknowledge that what the child is doing is difficult, but that they are right to confide in you.
- Reassure the child that they are not to blame.
- Make sure that, from the outset, you can understand what the child is saying.
- Be honest straight away and tell the child you cannot make promises that you will not be able to keep.
- Do not promise that you will keep the conversation a secret. Explain that you will need to involve other people and that you will need to write things down.
- Listen and believe the child; take them seriously.
- Do not allow your shock or distaste to show.
- Keep any questions to a minimum, but clarify any facts or words that you do not understand – do not speculate or make assumptions.
- Avoid closed questions (ie questions which invite yes/no answers).
- Do not probe for more information than is offered.
- Encourage the child to use their own words.
- Do not make negative comments about the alleged abuser.
- End the disclosure and ensure that the child is either being collected or is capable of going home on their own.
- Do not approach the alleged abuser.

Recording the Disclosure

Once the child has left, make an accurate written record of what was said. You may like to use the sample form on the following page as a template.

Once you have completed the written record:

- sign and date it
- provide copies for your manager, senior coach, club child protection officer and others as required
- store the information in accordance with your club/organisation or national governing body procedures.

Record of Disclosure

Name .... Date of Birth ....

Address ....

....

.... Postcode ....

Date .... Time .... Place ....

What the child has said:

Your own observations:

Any actions that you have decided to take:

Your Name .... Signature ....

Other Members of Staff Present

....

....

Dealing with Bullying

All incidents or suspicions of bullying must be taken very seriously. The guidelines in the panel below will help your club/organisation deal with the issue appropriately:

- Develop guidelines on dealing with bullying and ensure that these are part of an active policy.
- Promote the guidelines in your club's/organisation's code of practice.
- Ensure that the concepts of equity, values and inclusion are covered in staff training.
- Take all signs of bullying seriously.
- Involve parents and carers.
- Do not ignore the victim or the bully – encourage them to discuss their thoughts both with you and, if appropriate, with others within the group.
- Encourage the children involved to change their behaviour in order to improve the situation.
- Follow general guidelines – listen, record, report, reassure and take appropriate action.
- Invite professional organisations to explain specific issues to children and offer further help – this could be a session for both coaches and children.
- Share concerns – the victim may not be safe.
- Follow up what you do – remember that sport should be safe and fun for both the bully and the victim.

3.2 Responding to Observations

Children

Due to the nature of coaching, you have a unique opportunity to observe children both physically and emotionally. For example, it is now quite common for coaches to carry out a fitness assessment prior to the start of a coaching programme, during which personal details are recorded (eg height, weight and body measurements). These can prove useful if a child shows signs of rapid change through diet or weight training. However, always remember to obtain the consent of parents or carers to collect this kind of information when a child joins your club/organisation.

Colleagues

Remember, you not only have to consider the consequences of your own actions, but also those of others within your club/organisation. For example, from time to time, you may be required to observe other coaches' sessions and may spot risks that, for whatever reason, have been missed by the coach leading the session. In these circumstances, you may need to intervene, either by stopping the session or simply discussing your concerns with the coach in question. This should be viewed as good practice, rather than interfering, as failure to take action could result in a case of negligence being made against the coach. The incident should be recorded in writing and made available to other coaches to avoid them making the same mistake themselves.

Whereas some incidents are clearly a cause for concern and may prompt action such as a risk assessment, change to coaching style or review of goals, be aware that some incidents are not so obvious and only surface once the damage has occurred.

3.3 Sharing Your Concerns

As a result of a disclosure or an observation, you may be worried about what a child has said or simply have a *feeling* that something is not quite right. Taking action in cases of child abuse is never easy and you will inevitably experience a mixture of emotions. You may feel that you have been partly responsible; you may be worried about the consequences of the action you take for the child's family. These feelings are completely natural, particularly because of the media coverage of child abuse.

What is important is the child's long-term future – imagine what could happen if you do not take action. Sadly, a failure to act in some cases has led to a child's death, as many child abuse inquiries have shown. Your information could be vital in preventing further abuse and you have a responsibility to share and/or report your concerns, however small they may be. Many adult survivors of childhood abuse have said that telling someone who helped stop the abuse was a vital step in the healing process.

Sharing with a Senior Colleague/Line Manager

In some sport situations, it may be quite easy to determine who you should contact if you are concerned about a child being abused. For example, if you work for a local authority, in a sport or a leisure centre, at a school, or for your national governing body, you will have a senior colleague or line manager (the person to whom you are directly responsible/your employer/the person who appointed you). If your work with children takes place at a sports club, you may again be able to identify someone to whom you can report your concerns (eg the club secretary, chairperson). Whether you are a paid employee or volunteer, there should normally be someone to whom you can turn.

However, in some circumstances, particularly if you work in a voluntary capacity, there may be no obvious person to whom to report any concerns you may have. For example, you may coach at a club operating after school or on a Saturday morning for a local team. In this case, it is particularly important to plan what you would do if you suspected abuse, before you are actually faced with a real-life situation.

Remember!

Whoever you talk to, you will need to maintain confidentiality, but do not need to take full responsibility. Your senior colleague/line manager will expect to be informed so that you can begin to protect both the child and yourself in what could be a difficult situation.

Sharing with Parents/Carers

You should always be committed to working in partnership with parents or carers when there are concerns about their children. In most situations, it is therefore important to talk to parents or carers to help clarify any initial concerns. In doing so, you may discover reasons that explain behavioural changes or find out that the family needs further support. Parents and carers will usually inform someone at your club/organisation if their child is upset or unwell, but occasionally, this information may not reach you. In cases like this, simply talking to parents or carers can help to resolve any initial concerns.

If the concerns are about someone who also plays a role within sport, then the person in charge should inform the relevant sporting organisation's Child Protection Officer.

Sharing with Professionals

In some situations, particularly if it would be inappropriate to discuss your concerns with the child's parents or carers[1], it may be necessary to inform social services and/or the police. If available, your senior colleague/line manager should take responsibility for this. However, you need to be aware of what to do in case she is unavailable or inappropriate, or there is no-one obvious to whom to report your concerns. The process is as follows:

1. Inform the duty officer at social services or the police and explain that it involves child protection. Give your name, role, address and telephone number (this is helpful rather than required). Give clear, accurate details of the child (ie name, address and date of birth), what you have observed (include date and time, details of the child's behaviour and emotional state), what the child has said and what action you have taken.
2. Social services will advise you on what to do next and how and when to involve parents/carers, and will also take responsibility for ensuring that appropriate investigations are undertaken.
3. If a child needs urgent medical attention as a result of suspected abuse, then you must seek this as a matter of urgency. Inform social services as soon as possible to obtain advice about involving parents.
4. Record carefully what you have heard, seen and done.

1 See page 98 for further details.

Remember!

- However small your concern, share it with a senior colleague/line manager who will take responsibility for informing social services. If no senior colleague/line manager is available (or your concern is about him), then you must ring social services yourself, giving accurate details of your concerns.
- Social services departments have a responsibility to investigate all concerns of child abuse[1]; they do this jointly with the police[2]. This may involve talking to the child and their family and/or gathering more information.
- It is important to be open and honest with parents, but in some circumstances this may put the child in more danger[3]. If in doubt, discuss your concerns first with appropriate and qualified personnel.

1 See pages 102 to 103 for further details.

2 See page 103 for further details.

3 See page 98 for further details.

3.4 Dealing with Difficult Situations

Allegations against Parents/Carers

In some cases, a child may be placed at even greater risk if you share your concerns with his/her parents or carers (eg when a parent or carer may be responsible for the abuse or is not able to respond to the situation appropriately). In these circumstances, you must report any suspicion, allegation or incident of abuse to the person in charge as soon as possible, and ensure that it is recorded in writing. If the person in charge is not available, refer your concerns to social services or the police immediately.

Remember!

- Maintain confidentiality on a need to know basis only.
- Ensure the person in charge follows up with social services.
- Seek advice from your local social services officer about whether or not to consult the child's parents or carers.

Allegations Against Staff/Volunteers

As a coach, you are responsible for the welfare of each child in your care and for making others aware of their own responsibilities (eg volunteers helping out with trips, tours or social events). However, child abuse can and does occur outside the family setting, and it has occurred in sport.

Hearing allegations of child abuse against coaches, members of staff or volunteers is particularly distressing. It can raise feelings of anger because the children have placed their trust in adults who have abused that trust, and guilt on the part of other colleagues who may feel they could have done more to stop it happening.

Reporting suspicions, allegations or incidents of abuse against a colleague is equally distressing. Clubs/organisations should assure all coaches that they will fully support and protect anyone who, in good faith, reports his/her concern about a colleague's practice or the possibility that a child is being abused.

The diagram on page 99 outlines the action you should take if you are concerned about the behaviour of a member of staff or volunteer in your club/organisation. The same procedure applies in all cases, even if allegations are made some time after the event (eg by an adult who was abused as a child or about a member of staff who is still working with children).

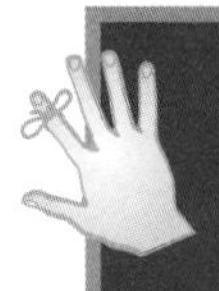

Remember!

The child will and should be at the centre of the whole process; their confidence, safety and security must be assured.

The diagram below offers some general guidelines on how to respond to any concerns you may have about staff or volunteers in your club/organisation. However, these guidelines are by no means definitive – you should also refer to your club's/organisation's policy.

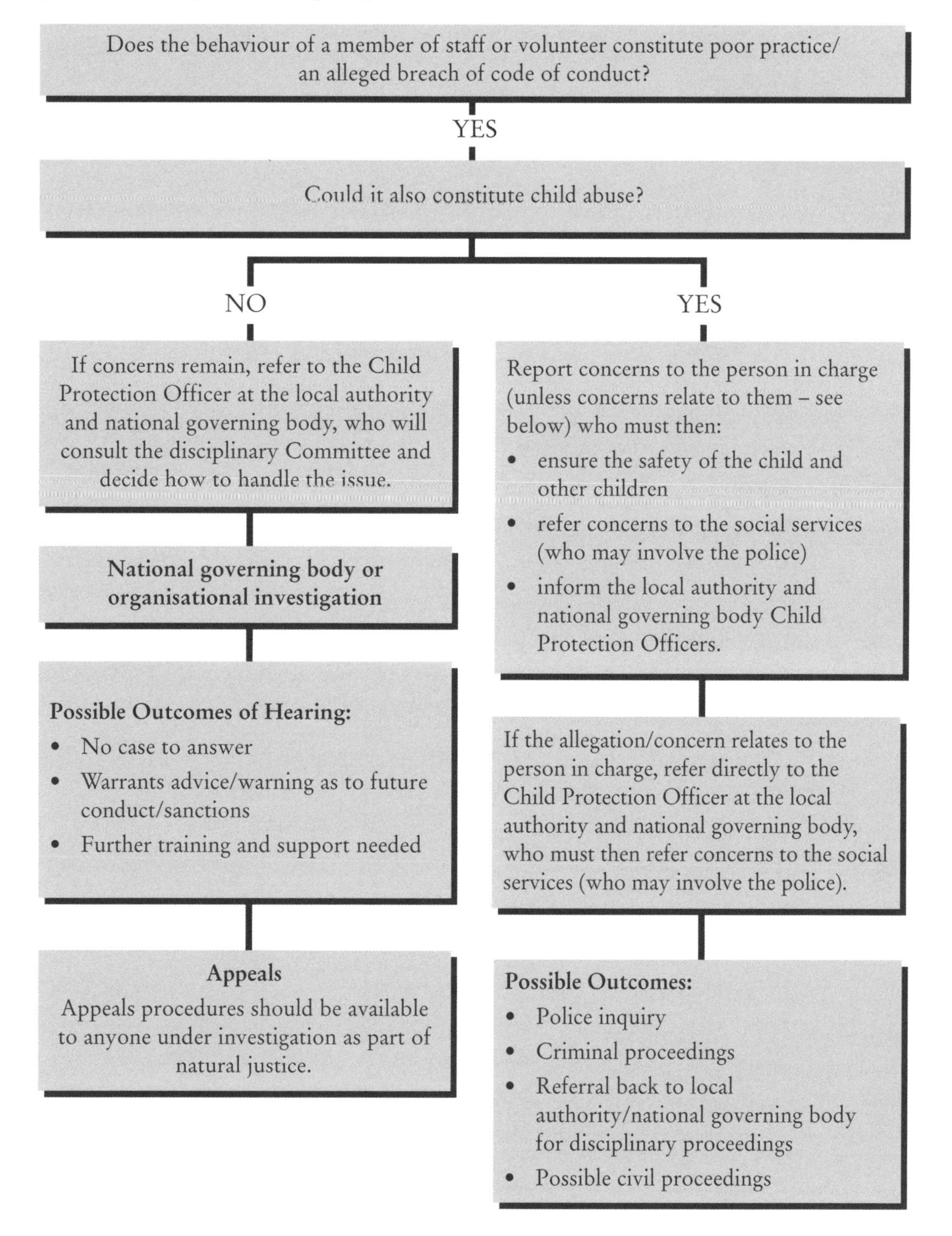

If you do not know who to turn to for advice or are worried about sharing your concerns with a senior colleague, contact social services directly (or the NSPCC on 0808-800 5000 or Childline on 0800-1111).

Figure 2: Responding to concerns about staff/volunteers

Allegations of abuse against members of staff in any setting can have far-reaching consequences. Other children may need to be interviewed by the police and social services. The effects on other staff can be distressing and child protection policies and recruitment/selection procedures may need to be reviewed.

There may be three types of investigation:

- Criminal
- Child protection
- Disciplinary.

Civil proceedings may also be initiated by the person, or family of the person, who reported the alleged abuse.

The club's/organisation's designated child protection officer (if available) should make his/her national governing body equivalent aware of the allegation and seek advice as appropriate (eg how to deal with the media). However, if the club's/organisation's child protection officer is the subject of the allegation, a senior person from the club/organisation should report directly to the national governing body's child protection officer.

The club/organisation and/or national governing body should make an immediate decision about whether an individual accused of abuse should be temporarily suspended from coaching pending further police and social services inquiries.

Irrespective of the findings of social services or police inquiries, the club/organisation must assess all individual cases under the appropriate misconduct/disciplinary procedure, to decide whether the accused can be reinstated and, if so, how this can be handled sensitively with other staff or volunteers. The welfare of children should always be the first point of consideration, even when there is insufficient evidence to uphold any action by the police or social services.

3.5 Responsibilities of Agencies/Organisations

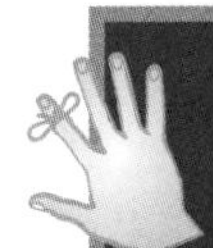

Remember!

If you suspect that a child may be being abused, it is not your responsibility to take control of the situation nor to decide whether or not child abuse is actually taking place. However, you do have a responsibility to ensure the safety of the children under your supervision. You should therefore inform the appropriate agencies/organisation of your concerns so that they can make enquiries and take any action that may be necessary to protect the child.

Your Club/Organisation

The last thing you should have to do when an incident of child abuse is suspected is to search through the telephone directory to find out who to contact. Your role at this time will be to reassure the child and act calmly – not to appear confused or unsure of what to do. Your club/organisation should therefore have a child protection policy and procedures document that explains the process to follow.

In addition, your club/organisation should identify a designated person to handle child protection issues. This person should complete a self-declaration form and undergo a voluntary police check for quality assurance purposes. The designated person will require support from your club/organisation and appropriate training. This support should be provided as part of the child protection policy and implementation procedures adopted by your club/organisation.

Processes and procedures are never solutions in themselves, but should always be adopted as a means of ensuring better outcomes for the children involved. No guidance can, or should, attempt to offer a detailed prescription of how to work with each individual child or family. Good practice calls for the effective cooperation between different agencies and professions.

National Governing Bodies

In recent years, national governing bodies have recognised the need to:

- publish child protection policies and codes of ethics and conduct
- address sensitive areas of manual handing during training sessions on the delivery of their sports
- protect coaches and provide advice in areas such as recruitment, insurance, first aid and resource use.

All national governing bodies are now required to have child protection policies and should also have a child protection officer/lead officer in child protection.

Local Authorities

In order to fulfil their social service responsibilities, local authorities have specific legal duties in respect of the Children Act 1989 and the Protection of Children Act 1999. Each local authority should work to safeguard the welfare of children in partnership with other public agencies, the voluntary sector and service users and carers. Local authorities have the leading responsibility to provide services for children in need, such as establishing an Area Child Protection Committee and ensuring that it functions effectively.

Local authorities are often involved in play scheme provision. You may be coaching in a play scheme either during a school holiday or for a specific programme. Many local authorities will provide the expertise of a community sports coordinator to make sure that all those involved in such coaching activities have access to the most appropriate resources, including coach education.

Detailed policies and procedures should also be available from all local authorities providing guidance on all aspects of good practice and child protection, including implementation plans for coaches to follow.

Social Services

Social services provide a wide range of care and support for adults, children and families. This includes older people; people with physical or learning disabilities; people with mental health or substance misuse problems; ex-offenders and young offenders; families, especially where children have special needs; children at risk of harm; children who need to be accommodated or looked after by the local authority, through fostering or residential care; children who are placed for adoption.

Social services have a statutory duty under the Children Act 1989 and Protection of Children Act 1999 to ensure the welfare of children and to work with the local Area Child Protection Committee to comply with its procedures. When a child protection referral is made, social services have a legal responsibility to investigate if they have reason to suspect that a child in their area is suffering, or likely to suffer significant harm.

A child who is at risk of significant harm will invariably be a child in need. Social services are responsible for coordinating an assessment of the:

- child's needs
- parents' capacity to keep the child safe
- parents' capacity to promote the child's welfare
- wider family circumstances.

This assessment will involve sharing information with the police and significant others (eg health or education authorities). Where the child is thought to be in immediate danger, social services may apply to the courts for an Emergency Protection Order which places the child under the protection of the local authority for a minimum of eight days.

Because of their responsibilities, duties and powers in relation to vulnerable children, social services act as the principle point of contact for children if there are child welfare concerns. They may also be contacted directly by parents, family members seeking help, concerned friends and neighbours and professionals, or others from statutory and voluntary agencies.

Police

The police recognise the fundamental importance of inter-agency working in combating child abuse. All forces have child protection units and, despite variations in their structure, they will normally take primary responsibility for investigating child abuse cases. They also have emergency powers to enter premises and ensure the immediate protection of children believed to be suffering from, or at risk of, significant harm. The police will determine whether criminal proceedings should be initiated.

Other Agencies/Organisations

A number of additional agencies/organisations can provide important routes for children in need into statutory and voluntary services – these include:

- Childline[1]
- NSPCC Helpline[2]
- education services
- cultural and leisure services
- health services
- day care services
- probation services
- prison service
- youth justice services
- voluntary and private sectors.

There may also be local support groups in your area that you could approach for guidance, support or practical help.

1 ChildLine is available for all children in trouble or in danger (tel: 0800-1111).

2 The NSPCC Helpline is primarily for adults who have concerns about children and offers confidential advice (tel: 0808-800 5000).

3.6 Taking Preparatory Action

It is important to be prepared for the possibility of having to deal with suspected abuse in the future, so that, in the event, you are able to respond calmly and appropriately.

The following action points relate to your club's/organisation's records and are things you should be able to tackle more or less immediately:

- Children's names:
  - Check that names are complete and spelt correctly.
  - Be aware that parents'/carers' surnames may be different to that of the children.
- Phone numbers:
  - Check that numbers are up to date and include area codes.
  - Check that mobile numbers are correct.
- Addresses:
  - Check that addresses are complete and up to date.
  - If possible, obtain a map of the local area – it is surprising how many people are unfamiliar with it.

ACTIVITY 26

Jot down any additional action points that you think would help you in the space provided below:

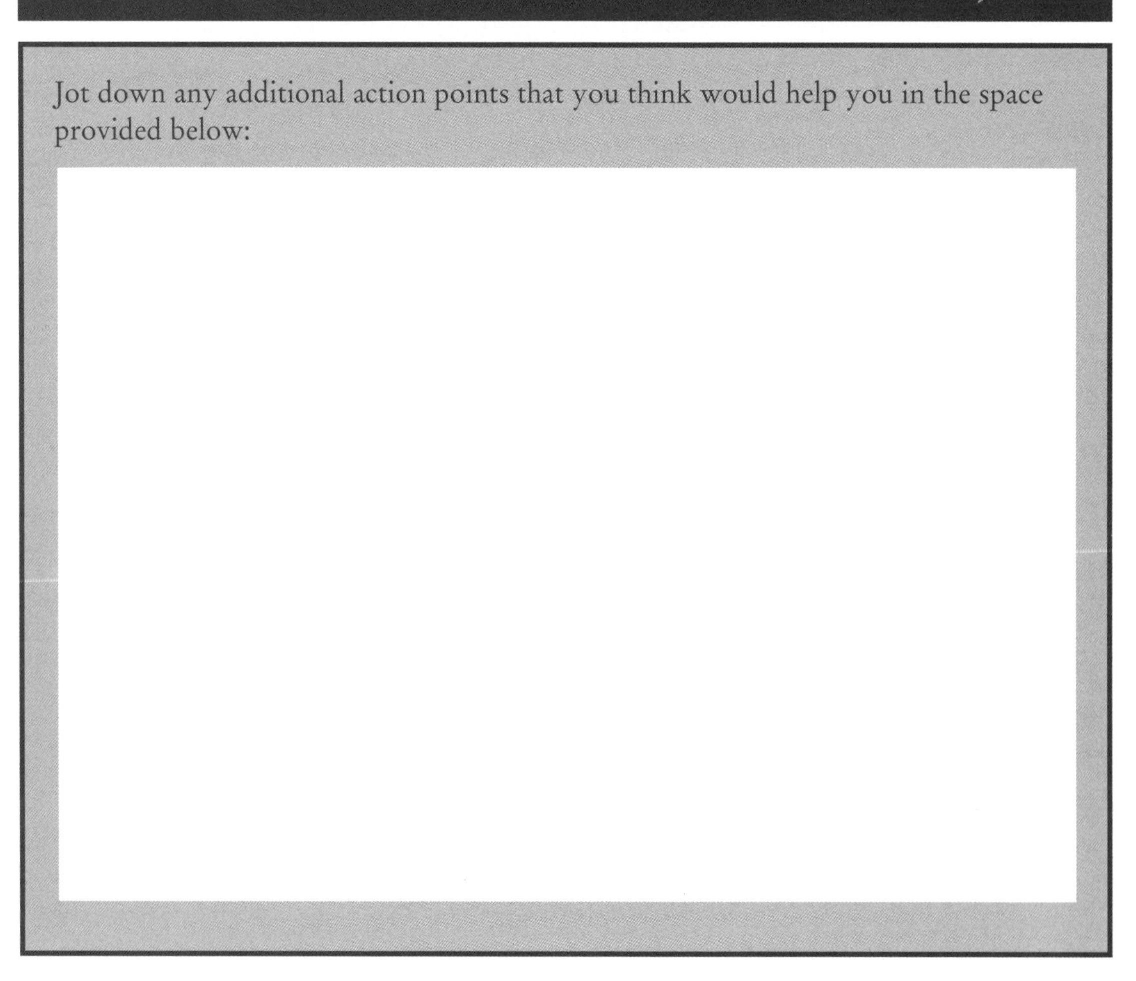

The following activity will help you compile a list of people to contact in relation to child protection issues. Take a photocopy of your completed list and keep it somewhere safe for future reference.

ACTIVITY 27

Find out the names and telephone numbers of the main child protection contacts within your club/organisation and/or national governing body, social services and the police, and record the details below.

Child Protection Contacts

Name of the person in your normal coaching environment to whom you should report any concerns about child protection issues:

....

Job Title: ....

Address: ....

....

....

Tel No: ....

Child Protection Officer: ....
(if different from above)

Tel No: ....

Social Services Contact: ....

Tel No: ....

Police Station Contact: ....

Tel No: ....

Name of Local Hospital: ....

Tel No: ....

Now turn over.

Feedback

You may have found this activity easy if you work in a club/organisation which has clear guidelines and procedures to follow when abuse is suspected, and a designated person to whom you can report your concerns (usually the head teacher, coach, most senior person). It is essential that this designated person is trained and knowledgeable about child protection. If you do not have one already, ask your club/organisation for a copy of its child protection procedures and jot down any further information that you think should be readily available.

However, you may have found the activity quite difficult if either your club/organisation does not currently have any clear procedures, or it does, but you are unaware of them. If this is the case, seek guidance from your employer (or, if you work in a voluntary capacity, the person responsible for your work) or contact your national governing body.

If you are self-employed (or work voluntarily) and work with children at a private venue (eg a gym club in the village hall, athletics session at a college track, football session on the church field, tennis lesson on a friend's private court), there may not be anyone to whom you can report your concerns. If you are in this situation, if there is no one else available or if you are the most senior person, ***you will have to take responsibility for taking the next step****. You will need to familiarise yourself with the recommended guidelines and draw up your own code of practice.*

You may or may not have obtained any specific guidelines. Whether you are part of a public, private or voluntary body, you have a duty of care for the children with whom you work. This means that every organisation should have a policy that clearly states that it is the duty of all those employed or involved to prevent the physical, sexual or emotional abuse of children with whom they come into contact.

What Would You Do?

In the following activities, you will be asked to consider a series of case studies and scenarios. In some cases, you will be asked to comment on the actions of the people involved; in others, you will be asked to think about how you would respond if you were involved. Remember that making the correct decision is not always straightforward. Refer to the information in this pack or contact more experienced professionals for advice and guidance.

ACTIVITY 28

Case Study 1

The following case study has been written from a parent or carer's point of view. As you read through it, jot down your concerns as a coach in the space provided.

Your children want to attend a sports team practice in your local park every Saturday morning. You agree that they can go and provide them with some money, sports kits and drinks. As the park is not far away and near to their school, you agree that they can walk there together unaccompanied and feel assured that they will be safe. The practice goes well, the children seem keen and the session is popular, with lots of other children and parents attending.

After a while, the enthusiastic coaches enter a local tournament. As a result of this, even more children turn up to practices, several teams are formed and a request is made to parents to provide a donation in order to buy equipment. You decide to go and watch a practice – you have not really thought to do so in the past and wish to see the set-up. However, you do not tell your children that you intend to turn up. On arriving at the park, you are disturbed to see lots of children playing sport, but no sign of your own. You spot an adult, but he is just another parent having a game. You begin to get very concerned and quite worried – it is time for the practice to end and still there is no sign of your children.

More parents gather and you learn that some of the children have been taken to play a match across the other side of town – in cars by other parents. You also learn that your children are in this team. Time passes very slowly. It is cold and you do not really know what to do; it begins to rain and there is no shelter. You have just about had enough, when out of a car step your children, who happily tell you that they won their match in extra time.

You are introduced to the coaches who turn out to be teenagers – they are in the sixth form at school and just love playing sport.

Continued ...

Your concerns:

ACTIVITY 28

Case Study 2

Now compare Case Study 1 with the following, which has also been written from a parent's or carer's perspective. As you read through it, jot down any examples of good practice that you come across in the space provided.

Your children want to take up sport on a Saturday morning. You are pleased because there is a well-established local club nearby. You telephone the organiser who sends you an information pack about the club, in which you are surprised, but pleased, to find several consent forms, a request for information about your children and a code of conduct which sets out the club objectives and code of practice for the coaches. You are asked to complete the documentation and are invited to take your children for a trial visit.

The following Saturday, you take the children to the club to meet a coach and receive an induction to the centre. You are all very impressed with what you see and are informed that recent lottery money has enabled the club to invest in coach training, resources and facilities. You are also told that, as members, you will have to be involved with the progress of your children and may be asked to contribute to some activities (eg supervising changing rooms, preparing refreshments, joining the club committee, being available for matches, fund-raising events and socials).

As you tour the club, you see that some of the younger coaches are working with more experienced ones and are impressed to learn that the club employs qualified staff and makes use of volunteers. The session ends and you see that all the children are collected by their parents. They appear pleased with the morning's training and are able to speak freely to staff. Both you and your children confirm that you wish to join the club.

Examples of good practice:

Now turn over.

Feedback

Both of these scenarios exist in practice. Case Study 1 shows how, for many, sport manages to exist. However, in this kind of set-up, an accident could be just waiting to happen. Fortunately, some clubs run on an informal basis like this one often develop and adopt the more formal structure of the club in Case Study 2.

Given the choice, the good practice illustrated in Case Study 2 should be the way forward. Parents and carers have the right to make these choices for their children. In turn, coaches have the opportunity to provide choices that make sport safe for children.

ACTIVITY 29

This activity is designed to help you check your understanding of good practice and the need for procedures. As you read through the following scenario, jot down any examples of good practice that you come across in the left-hand column of the table below. Then jot down any additional areas of good practice that you think should be adopted in the right-hand column.

As the manager of a local voluntary-run club, you are responsible for recruiting staff. Your committee has approved a proposal to recruit three extra part-time leisure activity staff. You also decide to take the opportunity to recruit volunteers at the same time. You decide to place an advert in the local paper, in which you outline the aims of the club and specific areas of coaching in which you wish to recruit staff. There is an excellent response to the advert, particularly from students at a local college.

As part of your pre-recruitment checks, you send out application forms accompanied by information outlining the qualities and experience required. You also ask candidates to submit a reference. You decide to formally interview several candidates to clarify their qualifications, training needs, previous experience and expectations. At the interviews, you explain that successful candidates will be required to receive training on working with children.

You appoint the three members of part-time staff and several volunteers. You explain that they will all receive an induction to the club and regular feedback on their progress.

Examples of Good Practice	Additional Recommendations

Now turn over.

Feedback

Every club/organisation should ensure that all reasonable steps are taken to prevent unsuitable people from working with children. This applies to both paid and unpaid staff.

The manager of this club made a concerted effort to recruit suitable staff. Examples of good practice include:

- *seeking approval from the club committee to recruit extra staff, as it is important that the committee is kept aware of all club activities*
- *ensuring that the advert contains relevant information about the club and the posts available – this will help to attract the right kind of people*
- *carrying out a formal application process and asking for references*
- *conducting formal interviews to assess the suitability of the candidates*
- *making all candidates aware of what will be expected of them*
- *providing successful candidates with a formal induction to the club and regular feedback on their progress.*

In addition to the above, the manager could have:

- *contacted the local college for background information on the students that applied for the posts*
- *asked applicants for two written references, instead of just one*
- *asked applicants to complete a self-declaration form or carried out a police check*
- *selected applicants with some or all of the following attributes: first aid training, child protection training, coaching experience, skill updates*
- *implemented formal monitoring and appraisal procedures for all club staff, particularly the new recruits.*

ACTIVITY 30

The following extracts are from a local sport and leisure club's records. For each one, decide what you would do if you were involved in the situation:

1. Staff complained that equipment, including trampolines, football goals and badminton posts, was not put away after being used, but just pushed into the corners of the sports hall. The storeroom in the sports hall was full of benches, chairs and cupboards.
2. One of the club's coaches raised concerns about the behaviour of a group of children attending his session. In the changing room, he discovered that shampoo had been poured into some of the children's bags, shoes had been placed in the shower and coats had been hidden in the outside bins. He was alerted to this by a parent who said that it was not the first time this had happened and that her child was unhappy and wished to leave the club. When questioned, none of the children said anything.
3. One of the senior coaches reported that he was not happy about a younger coach dating a 17-year-old performer. He knew that the relationship had been going on for some time.
4. Several children attending a sports session ending at 7.30pm were continually being left waiting by their parents until the TV soap operas finished at 8.30pm. The premises were locked at 8.00pm.
5. A member of staff asked other coaches whether they had noticed a difference in Sarah recently. At the beginning of the season, her weight had been normal for her age. However, she was now looking thin and tired, and often sat out of training sessions.
6. A fixture was abandoned due to the behaviour of the visiting team's parents on the sideline.
7. A risk assessment at the sport and leisure club revealed a substantial number of shredded cans on the grass pitches.
8. A coach noticed that one of the younger children had cigarette burns on his arms during an activity session in which children got hotter than usual and took their jumpers off. The child quickly covered the burns up and seemed very reluctant to discuss them.
9. A part-time coach started the season well, but soon slipped into a routine of arriving late and getting the children to set out equipment unsupervised.
10. Several parents felt uneasy about a stranger hanging around the club with a camera.

Now turn over.

Feedback

The extracts from the club's records all describe incidents which, if left, could have become far more serious and placed children in danger of physical, emotional and sexual abuse, or neglect.

Fortunately, the club in question had procedures in place to minimise any damaging or harmful effects in the event of a situation arising in which abuse could occur.

Further ongoing actions could include:

- *minimising opportunities for an adult to be left alone with a single child*
- *providing opportunities for coaches to talk to parents and carers about the expected standards of behaviour of young performers*
- *arranging for coaches to meet children with their parents and carers present*
- *coaches encouraging parents and carers to attend training sessions and to support competitions*
- *carrying out random checks on coaching practice*
- *encouraging parents and carers to take greater responsibility for ensuring the safety of their child*
- *introducing a system enabling children to talk to an independent person outside the club – this person should be given clear written guidelines on the action to take if abuse is disclosed or suspected*
- *applying agreed procedures for protecting children to all staff (whether paid or voluntary, full- or part-time, permanent or temporary). This should include:*
  - *ensuring that all staff have clear roles and responsibilities*
  - *issuing guidelines on the action to take if abuse is disclosed or suspected*
  - *implementing a supervision and appraisal system that monitors roles and relationships, and observes coaching practice.*

Measures such as these not only protect the children, but also protect coaches from accusations of improper behaviour.

3.7 Summary

In this section, you have been offered guidance on how to cope if you suspect a child is being abused and on the policies and procedures your club/organisation should establish in order to promote good practice and protect children.

Remember!

- The welfare of the child must be of paramount importance in all issues relating to child protection.
- Talk to parents or carers to clarify any injury or change in behaviour (unless the allegations concern sexual abuse or the child might be placed at increased risk).
- If you are still concerned, contact the duty officer at social services or the police. If a coach is involved, inform your national governing body as well.
- Give clear accurate details, child's name, address and reasons for your concern.
- Social services will advise you about what to do next and will take responsibility for ensuring appropriate investigations are undertaken if necessary.
- If a child needs urgent medical attention as a result of suspected abuse, you must seek this as a matter of urgency, then inform social services or the police. Seek advice from social services before informing parents.
- Record carefully what you have seen, heard and done as soon as possible.
- Remember too that confidentiality in matters relating to child protection is vital, and information must only be shared with senior colleagues (where essential) and child protection professionals.

Remember not to shoulder the burden of child protection on your own. If you are concerned or unsure, always ring social services, the police or the NSPCC. Their telephone numbers are in the local phone book. The NSPCC offers a free 24-hour National Child Protection Helpline (tel: 0808-800 5000).

There may be issues that you need to discuss with your national governing body, employer or organisation – ensure that you make arrangements to meet the appropriate personnel.

If you require further information or confidential advice (for professional or personal reasons), Section Four (pages 117–122) provides an extensive list of useful contacts and recommended further reading in relation to child protection issues.

Section 4

Where Next?

4.0 Introduction

Part of being a good coach is being open to new ideas and training and, to some extent, being aware that you need updating in certain areas. It is also about understanding the needs of the people you are coaching and accepting advice on how to accommodate them. If you have not already done so, you are strongly recommended to attend **scUK's** Coach Workshop *Good Practice and Child Protection*[1]. This section provides a comprehensive list of publications, workshops and organisations that can provide support and guidance on child protection issues.

4.1 Further Reading

This section lists a selection of useful publications and workshops that support the information provided in this pack. It is divided into subsections to make it easier to find the resource(s) you are looking for.

Sport-specific

Brackenridge, C (2001) **Spoilsports: understanding and preventing sexual exploitation in sport**. London, Routledge. ISBN 041925 7705

Earle, C (2003) **How to Coach Children in Sport**, Leeds, **sports coach UK**, ISBN 1902523539

Kerr, A (1999) **Protecting disabled children and adults in sport and recreation: the guide.** London, Disability Sport England. ISBN 1 902523 18 0

sports coach UK (2001) **Code of conduct for sports coaches**. Leeds, Coachwise Ltd.

sports coach UK (updated 2001) **Safe and sound** (leaflet). Leeds, Coachwise Ltd.

Sports Council for Northern Ireland (1998) **Child protection fact file**. Belfast, Sports Council for Northern Ireland.

UK Sport (2000) **UK vision for coaching**. Leeds, Coachwise Ltd.

1 For further details, contact your local Regional Training Unit (see page 119 for contact details) or visit www.sportscoachuk.org

General

Armstrong, H (1997) **Taking care**. London, National Children's Bureau. ISBN 1874 579 857

Bannister, A (ed) (1992) **From hearing to healing: working with the aftermath of child sexual abuse**. London, Longmans. ISBN 0582 091 454

Blagg, H, Hughes, JA and Wattam, C (1989) **Child sexual abuse: listening, hearing and validating the experiences of children**. London, Longmans. ISBN 0582 056 470

Child Care (1995) **Our duty to care**. Belfast, Child Care.

Creighton, S (1992) **Child abuse trends in England and Wales, 1988-90**. London, NSPCC. ISBN 0902 498 363

Department of Health (2001) **Children and young people on child protection registers**. Great Britain, Department of Health. ISBN 1841 824 372

DHSSNI (1995) **The children (NI) order**. Northern Ireland, Department of Health and Social Services.

Elliot, M (1986) **Keeping safe: a practical guide to talking with children**. 3rd edition. London, Bedford Square Press/NCVO. ISBN 0348 026 912

Elliot, M (1993) **Protecting children**. London, HMSO.

Glaser, D and Frost, S (1993) **Child sexual abuse**. 2nd edition. London, Macmillan. ISBN 03 33 576 020

Herbert, M (1993) **Children and the Children Act**. London, Bedford Square Press.

HMSO (1999) **Working together to safeguard children**. London, HMSO. ISBN 0 11 321 4723

Home Office (1993) **Safe from harm**. London, Home Office Publications. ISBN 08625 2993 X

Home Office (1999) **Caring for young people and the vulnerable? Guidance for preventing abuse of trust**. London, Home Office.

Jones, D and Pickett, J (eds) (1987) **Understanding child abuse**. 2nd edition. London, Macmillan Educational Publications. ISBN 03 33 428 935

NSPCC (2000) **Child maltreatment in the United Kingdom: a study of the prevalence of child abuse and neglect**. London, NSPCC. ISBN 1 84228 006 6

Stainton Rogers, W, Hevey, D and Ash, E (1989) **Child abuse and neglect: facing the challenge**. London, Open University Press. ISBN 0713 462 167

Wescott, HL (1993) **The abuse of children and adults with disabilities**. NSPCC, London. ISBN 0902 498 401

4.2 sports coach UK Contacts

sports coach UK
114 Cardigan Road
Headingley
Leeds
LS6 3BJ
Tel: 0113-274 4802
Fax: 0113-275 5019
E-mail: coaching@sportscoachuk.org
Website: www.sportscoachuk.org

Details of all **sports coach UK** (and former National Coaching Foundation) publications are available from:

Coachwise 1st4sport
Chelsea Close
Off Amberley Road
Armley
Leeds
LS12 4HP
Tel: 0113-201 5555
Fax: 0113-231 9606
E-mail: enquiries@1st4sport.com
Website: www.1st4sport.com

For general information about **sports coach UK** workshops, contact the Workshop Booking Centre on 0845-601 3054. For details of workshops running in your area, contact your nearest Regional Training Unit or home countries office. RTU contact details are available from **sports coach UK**.

4.3 Other Useful Contacts

This section lists a selection of organisations that can provide support and guidance on child protection issues. It is divided into subsections to make it easier to find the organisation(s) you are looking for.

Confidential Helplines

If this pack has raised personal issues for you, the following organisations will be able to offer confidential help and advice:

- **The Albany Trust** (Tel: 020-8767 1827)
  One-to-one counselling for people who have been sexually abused or suffer from psychological difficulties.
- **NSPCC Helpline** (Tel: 0808-800 5000)
  Telephone helpline for adults who are concerned that a child has been abused, and counselling for adults and children who have been abused.
- **ChildLine** (Tel: 0800-1111)
  Confidential telephone advice for children who are being abused or are at risk.
- **Contact Youth** (Tel: 028-9045 7847)
  Youth counselling.
- **Nexus Institute** NI (Tel: 028-9032 6803)
  Counselling for adult survivors of sexual abuse.
- **Local Rape Crisis Centres**
  Can offer help to survivors of abuse. You will find the number of your local centre in the telephone directory.
- **Child Protection in Sport Unit** (CPSU) (Tel: 0116-234 7278/7280)
  Serves as a point of contact for sports clubs/organisations in relation to child protection issues in sport.

National Sports Councils

In addition to seeking the advice of the national governing body in your sport, the following organisations will also be able to offer help and advice:

Sport England
16 Upper Woburn Place
London
WC1H OQP
Tel: 020-7273 1500
Fax: 020-7383 5740
E-mail: info@sportengland.org
Website:www.sportengland.org

sportscotland
Caledonia House
South Gyle
Edinburgh
EDH12 9DQ
Tel: 0131-317 7200
Fax: 0131-317 7202
E mail: gen.info@sportscotland.org.uk
Website:www.sportscotland.org.uk

Sports Council for Northern Ireland
House of Sport
Upper Malone Road
Belfast
BT9 5LA
Tel: 028-9038 1222
Fax: 028-9068 2757
E-mail: info@sportscouncil-ni.org.uk
Website:www.sportni.org

Sports Council for Wales
Sophia Gardens
Cardiff
CF11 9SW
Tel: 029-2030 0500
Fax: 029-2030 0600
E-mail: scw@scw.co.uk
Website: www.sports-council-wales.co.uk

UK Sport
40 Bernard Street
London
WC1N 1ST
Tel: 020-7841 9500
E-mail: info@uksport.gov.uk
Website: www.uksport.gov.uk

Other Organisations

Criminal Records Bureau
PO Box 91
Liverpool
L69 2UH
Tel: 0870-90 90 811
Website: www.crb.gov.uk

Child Protection in Sport Unit
NSPCC National Training Centre
3 Gilmour Close
Beaumont Leys
Leicester
LE4 1EZ
Tel: 0116-234 7278/7280
Fax: 0116-234 0464
E-mail: cpsu@nspcc.org.uk
Website: www.sportprotects.org.uk

Department of Health, Social Services and Public Safety Northern Ireland
Castle Buildings
Stormont
Belfast
BT4 3SJ
Tel: 028-9052 0500
Fax: 028-9052 0572
Website: www.dhsspsni.gov.uk

Disclosure Scotland
Disclosure Bureau
1Pacific Quay
Glasgow
G51 1EA
Tel: 0141-585 8495
Website: www.scro.police.uk

NSPCC
Weston House
42 Curtain Road
London
EC2A 3NH
Tel: 020-7825 2500
Fax: 020-7825 2525
Website: www.nspcc.org.uk

SPRITO
24-32 Stephenson Way
London
NW1 2HD
Tel: 020-7388 7755
Fax: 020-7388 9733
E-mail: the.nto@sprito.org.uk
Website: www.sprito.org.uk

Appendix A

Criminal Records Bureau – Guidelines[1]

What is the Criminal Records Bureau?

The Criminal Records Bureau (CRB) has been set up by the Home Office to improve access to criminal record checks for employment-related and voluntary appointment purposes. In particular, it will provide protection for children and other vulnerable people against those who might wish to harm them.

Some sporting clubs/organisations already require police checks on those involved in sport with young people[2]. As recommended in Section 1.3 of this pack (see page 18), all sport and leisure providers should adopt this practice as part of an overall child protection policy.

Given the number of adults involved in either a paid or voluntary capacity in sporting clubs/organisations, obtaining, processing and storing the information will be a huge task. The aim of this appendix is to give guidance to sports clubs/organisations and national governing bodies on how to approach this.

When Should Someone be Checked?

The CRB provides a service to employers and volunteering groups in England and Wales[3] of all kinds called *Disclosure*. The employer will be able to use the Disclosure service to help establish whether a successful candidate has a background that might make them unsuitable for the position in question.

1 Adapted with kind permission from the Criminal Records Bureau and the Child Protection in Sport Unit.

2 While the information provided by the CRB is important in terms of recruitment and selection, organisations must recognise that this is only one of a much wider series of steps that need to be taken in order to create and sustain a safe environment for children. These steps are outlined in Sections One, Two and Three of this pack.

3 For information about Disclosure services in Scotland, telephone 0141-585 8495 or visit www.scro.police.uk, and in Northern Ireland, telephone 028-9052 0500 or visit www.dhsspsni.gov.uk

As well as using this service to check the background of new candidates, clubs/organisations should consider whether existing staff or volunteers should also be checked. This is especially important if an individual is being considered for a change in role that increases their contact with children.

This procedure will need to be implemented carefully within a club/organisation and may require amendments to current national governing body constitutions. It is important that the context for this action is fully communicated to all those involved in the sport and that issues of confidentiality are fully detailed. You will need to consider who within the national governing body will communicate this to staff and volunteers, and who will hold the information and make sure that this process complies with Data Protection Legislation.

One option that you may wish to consider is using a declaration as a means of implementing this procedure, such as the following statement:

From (date), the governing body of (sport) adopted a child protection policy. This policy will ensure that (sport) takes all necessary steps to promote a safe atmosphere for all those children and young people involved in (sport). All those currently involved with (sport) with significant contact with children will be required to give an assurance that they have no previous criminal convictions that could put children at risk. This information is ***strictly confidential*** *except for the legal obligation of reporting child abuse.*

The applicant initiates the Disclosure check and both the applicant and the employer receive copies of the Disclosure. You may wish to notify applicants of your intention to seek a Disclosure. A suggested statement to be included on all application forms is:

This post involves substantial access to children. As a club/organisation, we are committed to the welfare and protection of children. All applications to work with us in either a voluntary or paid capacity will involve a Criminal Records Bureau check.

If a club/organisation knowingly appoints a person where a ban exists, they will be committing a criminal offence. Under the Protection of Children Act 1999, voluntary clubs/organisations are encouraged to report their concerns while registered children's clubs/organisations are obliged to report concerns.

Level of Disclosure

It will be up to each applying body to determine what is the appropriate level of Disclosure. The following table is designed to give guidance as to what level is appropriate. The CRB will provide three levels of Disclosure:

Level of Disclosure	What Checks Are Provided?	Who Would This Be Appropriate For?
Basic Disclosure	Unspent convictions.	Those working with the club in a position that brings them into indirect contact with children (eg fund-raisers, ticket sellers).
Standard Disclosure	All convictions, cautions, reprimands or warnings plus information held by the Department of Health (DH) and Department for Education and Skills (DfES).	Those working directly with children who are **always** under the direct supervision of a senior official.
Enhanced Disclosure	All above checks plus an extra level of checking with local police force records.	Any individuals involved in a position offering significant direct contact with children (ie those in sole charge such as club coaches, teachers, team managers).

Please note: applications for the Standard and Enhanced Disclosures can only be made through a body that is registered with the CRB. The registered body must adhere to the CRB Code of Practice and ensure confidentiality. When a Disclosure is issued, a copy of this will be sent to both the registered body and the individual concerned. At some point in the future, any individual will be able to seek a Basic Disclosure for themselves.

More detailed information is available from the CRB and the Child Protection in Sport Unit (CPSU) at the following addresses:

Criminal Records Bureau
PO Box 91
Liverpool
L69 2UH
Tel: 0870-90 90 811
Website: www.crb.gov.uk

Child Protection in Sport Unit
NSPCC National Training Centre
3 Gilmour Close
Beaumont Leys
Leicester
LE4 1EZ
Tel: 0116-234 7278/7280
Fax: 0116-234 0464
E-mail: cpsu@nspcc.org.uk
Website: www.sportprotects.org.uk

Appendix B

National Occupational Standards for Coaching, Teaching and Instructing

The National Occupational Standards for Coaching, Teaching and Instructing (NOS) are based around a number of competences associated with planning, delivering and evaluating coaching sessions and programmes. The standards are used as part of national governing bodies' coach education awards and as the definition of competence for Scottish/National Vocational Qualifications (S/NVQs) in coaching, teaching and instructing. S/NVQs at Levels 2 and 3 are available in a number of sports. **sports coach UK** (**scUK**) has developed its Coach Development Programme around these standards. **scUK** workshops and packs aim to provide the underpinning knowledge for coaches who wish to meet the competences of the standards. They also give coaches guidelines on how to apply this knowledge to their coaching practice.

Protecting Children: A Guide for Sportspeople has been designed to support the following unit of the Level 2/3 NOS:

Unit	**C36 Support the protection of children from abuse**
C36.1	Report signs of possible abuse
C36.2	Respond to a child's disclosure of abuse

For further information about the National Occupational Standards for Coaching, Teaching and Instructing at Level 2/3, contact **scUK** or SPRITO at the following addresses:

sports coach UK
114 Cardigan Road
Headingley
Leeds
LS6 3BJ
Tel: 0113-274 4802
Fax: 0113-275 5019
E-mail: coaching@sportscoachuk.org
Website: www.sportscoachuk.org

SPRITO
24 Stephenson Way
London
NW1 2HD
Tel: 020-7388 7755
Fax: 020-7388 9733
E-mail: the.nto@sprito.org.uk
Website: www.sprito.org.uk